The Chinese Market

The Chinese Market

Entry Methods & Investment Strategies

Danai Krokou

BEP

BUSINESS EXPERT PRESS

Leader in applied, concise business books

The Chinese Market: Entry Methods & Investment Strategies

First published in 2021 by
Business Expert Press, LLC
222 East 46th Street, New York, NY 10017
www.businessexpertpress.com

ISBN-13: 978-1-63742-032-4 (paperback)
ISBN-13: 978-1-63742-033-1 (e-book)

Business Expert Press International Business Collection

Collection ISSN: 1948-2752 (print)
Collection ISSN: 1948-2760 (electronic)

First edition: 2021

10 9 8 7 6 5 4 3 2 1

To all of you who dare and take risks. . .

China has telescoped in one generation what other countries took centuries to achieve. No country has managed to accomplish so much in such a short time. China's unique attempt to complete two transitions at once—from a command to a market economy and from a rural to an urban society, is without historical precedent.

—The World Bank, *China 2020: Development and Challenges in the New Century*

Description

With its dual appeal as the world's factory and the largest consumer market worldwide, China is about to become the preferred playing field for American and European businesses with global ambitions. China's massive global development project, the Belt and Road Initiative (BRI), now includes more than two-thirds of the world's countries. In the coming years, the most promising entrepreneurs and most ambitious companies will be growing in China, with China. *Entering the Chinese Market* aims to assist Western businesses and entrepreneurs to understand and effectively enter the Chinese market. An essential factor for the success of investors and professionals engaging in business in or with China is being able to understand and correctly set up a sustainable and effective corporate structure. This book discusses different company structures, their functions, and their respective liabilities and provides practical and operational observations.

The book details all applicable decision-making processes to help you choose the most suitable structure based on your business scope, specific needs, and available capital when entering China. In addition, it discusses all relevant rules, regulations, documentation, and management issues related to the establishment of different types of structures such as WFOEs (wholly foreign-owned enterprises), representative offices (ROs), joint ventures (JVs), and other forms of investment. Topics covered in *Entering the Chinese Market* also include tax, legal, intellectual property rights, common pitfalls, and ways to address them.

Keywords

China investment; company structure; WFOE; U.S.–China joint ventures; U.S.–EU joint ventures China business; China investment; Chinese market; China strategy; China corporate structure; entry methods; market entry

Contents

Author's Statement

China is the uncontested El Dorado of the 21st century. The rapid rise of China as a leading economic power within a time frame of about three decades is often described by financial analysts as one of the greatest economic success stories of modern times. The story of the Western world's fascination with China dates back more than two millennia and began with a product that remains the symbol of this relationship: silk. Silk gave rise to the first myth of Chinese trade and the perception of the Silk Road as the main commercial avenue of antiquity. In recent decades, China's economic growth has been accelerating at speeds the world has not witnessed since the 19th-century Industrial Revolution. With its dual appeal as the world's factory and the largest consumer market worldwide, China has become the preferred playing field for businesses with global ambitions. In the next coming years the world's most promising entrepreneurs and most ambitious companies will be growing in China, with China.

While there are still important challenges for Western businesses operating in China, the business environment and market access for foreigners has significantly improved over the last decades. China climbed the World Bank ease of doing business ranking by 15 places in 2019. It now ranks higher than many European countries. China has evolved into a dynamic, fast-paced environment offering a plethora of opportunities to challenge-driven companies and business adventurers. It has emerged as one of the most aggressive countries promoting 5G technology (the fifth generation of cellular network technology) and is predicted to become the world's largest 5G market by 2025. China's strategy for achieving global technological dominance manifests throughout the country's signature foreign policy, the Belt and Road Initiative (BRI), an externally oriented development program designed to increase China's presence and investments in countries around the globe and to expand markets for Chinese products. Sustained high growth rates over the past several years have been rapidly transforming China into an industrialized economy. The current downturn is the first of such magnitude since the 2008 financial crisis. Back then, considerable reductions in production were recorded for four consecutive quarters after the crisis, but exceptionally high increases were also reported in subsequent quarters. It remains to be seen whether the COVID-19-induced economic crisis will follow a similar growth pattern. With the advent of coronavirus, the challenges and uncertainties that dominated previous years such as higher trade barriers and Brexit have clearly moved to the background. COVID-19 has forced governments to intervene in the world economy. While the full impact of the containment measures remains uncertain, in the beginning of 2021 China's economic recovery is gaining momentum. While much of the world continues to struggle with the virus, China's recovery has been relatively speedy. One of the most encouraging parts of China's recovery has been the recent rebound in consumer spending. At the same time, Joe Biden's presidency is expected to follow a more rational approach to bilateral trade between the United States and China. While political tensions—due to the recent human rights abuse in Western Xinjiang and the erosion of freedoms in semi-autonomous Hong Kong—are expected to continue, Biden's administration is expected to return to rules-based, free-market trade relations with China.

Entering the Chinese Market aims to assist Western entrepreneurs, businesses, and investors to understand and successfully enter the Chinese market. It is designed to work as a step-by-step guide to those businesses seeking to understand the investment strategies available to foreign companies operating in China and remain competitive in the tremendously challenging and profitable market that is China at the start of the third decade of the 21st century. My book *Entering the Chinese e-Merging Market* focused on the procedures and strategies that Western companies need to follow in order to enter China's electronic market, a process that requires smaller amounts of investment. *Entering the Chinese Market* is a concise and pragmatic guide of use to anyone considering to expand or set up a business entity in China. It contains practical advice, suggestions, key models, updated data, and strategies for different types of companies as well as alternative entry strategies using third jurisdictions such as Hong Kong or Singapore. It details all applicable decision-making processes to help you choose the most suitable structure based on your company's needs, business scope, and available capital. In addition, it discusses all relevant rules, regulations, documentation, and management issues related to the establishment of different types of structures such as WFOEs (wholly foreign-owned enterprises), ROs (representative offices), JVs (joint ventures), as well as other forms of investment. Topics covered in this book also include tax, legal, intellectual property rights (IPR), common pitfalls, and other vital issues facing Western investors who plan to enter China's thriving market.

Considering the country's rocky business environment, its uniquely complex legal, social, and political climate, and the recent COVID-19 crisis, China is a tough place to conduct business without the right preparation and planning. Even some of the world's largest and most successful companies stumbled hard when they tried to enter China. The process of setting up a business entity in China involves several steps, requires a well-planned strategy, and a great deal of organization, commitment, patience, and motivation. Finding the right strategy for your company is key. To achieve this it is crucial to know how the market really works and what role the Chinese government plays in the way your business functions. Always be ready to reconsider and adjust your strategy in order to respond to this fast-changing market. During the initial stages you might face one of the most unexpected challenges and brutal negotiations you have ever experienced. Remember that if you really want to succeed in China you must play by the local rules and do business the Chinese way.

The book begins with a general overview of the current Chinese market environment and presents in detail the various investment options available to different companies based on their business scope, available capital, and specific needs. It follows up with a detailed description of all available entry methods Western companies can use to establish a suitable business entity in China. Next, I move to an overview of relevant laws and regulations, practical challenges, emerging trends, as well as alternative strategy options. Finally, I conclude with recommendations on key strategies for different types of companies and a decision-making flowchart which many of my clients have found particularly useful. In the last section I have included useful links and a recommended reading list. All sums of money are expressed in Chinese Renminbi (RMB) and where helpful in U.S. dollars (U.S.$). Exchange rates are those prevailing at the year of the transactions referred to.

Besides providing you with information and advice on the best way to enter the Chinese market, an important message I want to convey through this book is that China is a market that Western companies simply cannot ignore and since you cannot beat it, you'd better join it. Chances are that many of your competitors are already in China and, more importantly, the country is now producing new its own international competitors as an increasing number of domestic Chinese companies grow and expand globally.

Introduction

China is big. As it grows bigger in population, it gains in complexity. In recent years, the country has emerged as a major global economic and trade power. China is currently the world's largest trading economy, largest manufacturer, largest holder of foreign exchange reserves, second largest economy, and second largest destination for foreign direct investment (FDI). For several years you have been reading all the hype about China's economic and political rise, its voracious appetite for technology, investment, services, imported commodities, and goods. You have also been hearing one breathless account after another about China's rise up the value chain and its steady march into international markets. If you add it all up, the conclusion in business terms becomes inescapable: every ambitious company regardless of size and business scope must consider the benefits of establishing its presence in China.

A look at any indicator, whether its investment figures, trade volumes, economic growth rates, or consumption patterns, shows that business in China is growing in size, opportunities, as well as complexity. Despite the fact that, until recently, China was viewed mainly as a low-cost manufacturing supply haven, it now offers tremendous market opportunities. With local wage rates rising rapidly every year, other Southeast Asian countries are stepping to fill the role of "world factory," while China is busy shaping its economic growth at home and abroad, according to its 14th Five-Year Plan (FYP) and the Belt and Road Initiative (BRI) discussed in later chapters.

However, market size isn't everything and just because something is big does not necessarily mean it is right for everyone. In fact, among the most common pitfalls facing foreign companies in China is the tendency to make generalizations and this is something you will have to be very careful about every step of the way, starting with the first big decision on whether your company really needs to be in China at all. Many companies or entrepreneurs seeking to enter China are wondering about the best opportunity available to their company or their business idea in China. Business executives and investors are often not clear about what the opportunities are, let alone how to develop them. You will have to sit down and do thorough research to understand the opportunities for your business. The aim of this book is to help guide you to make more informed decisions about your business opportunities in China.

Prior to the initiation of radical economic reforms and trade liberalization several decades ago, China maintained policies that kept the economy centrally controlled, poor, isolated from the global economy, and vastly inefficient. China has been among the world's fastest growing economies since it opened up to foreign trade and investment and since it started implementing free market reforms back in 1979. Some economists forecast that China will overtake the United States as the world's largest economy in the next few years. However, the ability of China to maintain a long-term growth will largely depend on the ability of the Chinese government to implement further economic reforms that will hasten the country's transition to a free market economy. The Chinese government has already acknowledged that the current economic growth model is unsustainable in the long term and has announced measures aimed at addressing economic challenges the country is facing: rebalancing of the Chinese economy by making domestic consumption the main engine of economic growth instead of relying solely on fixed investments and exports, boosting innovation and productivity, addressing the growing income disparities across the country, as well as enhancing environmental protection.

In November 2013, the Communist Party of China held the 3rd Plenum of its 18th Party Congress, during which a communiqué was issued, outlining a number of broad policy statements to be implemented by 2020. Many of the proposed measures were aimed at boosting the economic efficiency and competition. For instance, one of the statements of the communiqué was that the market would now play a "decisive" role when it comes to allocating resources in the economy. Foreign companies do no longer choose to go to China simply to reduce their production costs but they are also looking at getting a part of the fast-growing domestic market. For foreign entrepreneurs and investors this transformation of China presents tremendous opportunities. With little or no growth in many nations of the West and the pull of Chinese domestic consumption, the profile of Western companies investing in China is quickly expanding. China is about to experience a "second wave" of foreign investment. The first came mainly from large multinationals, while this new second wave brings with it greater amounts of investment from small and medium enterprises.

Conventional wisdom that only large multinational companies can do business in China is but a thing of the past. Although China is often seen as the Wild West in certain areas and far from meeting Western standards with respect to laws and business ethics, the country has come a long way and it now possesses the necessary building blocks to achieve further growth: an advanced banking and financial infrastructure, a huge number of consumers, and a growing Western-educated and English-speaking workforce.

Big transformations have marked the last 20 years: China's entry into the World Trade Organization (WTO), the explosion of China's middle class, the growth of the Internet, the Chinese government's willingness to open the country's business borders to the rest of the world, and most importantly, an increasingly market-driven economy that is about to overtake that of the United States. Business leaders throughout the West are well aware that China now offers potentially the most attractive investment environment worldwide, serving up a balanced mix of a consistently healthy gross domestic product (GDP) annual growth rate, political stability, newly opened industry sectors, an explosive consumer wealth, as well as a fast-developing, skilled, and educated local workforce. For a growing number of businesses and entrepreneurs this dramatic economic transformation means one thing: China is a must-win market. The country is critical not only as a manufacturing base for exports but most importantly as a destination market itself.

From 1979, when the first reforms began, until 2019, China's real GDP grew at an average annual rate of about 10 percent. It is estimated that 500 million people have been raised out of extreme poverty to date. In 2019 there were 1.58 million millionaires with personal wealth over 10 million Yuan in China. The Chinese government views a prosperous economy as a vital component of social stability and has expressed its desire to achieve more balanced economic development by moving away from the current economic model of "fast growth at any cost" to a "smarter" economic growth. One of the government's top priorities is to reduce reliance on energy-intensive and high-polluting industries by relying more on high-technology services and green energy.

It is a fact that the global economic crisis that began in 2008 has considerably affected China's economy. As a result, China's imports, exports, and FDI inflows declined; the country's GDP growth slowed while millions of Chinese workers lost their jobs. The government responded by implementing a $586 billion stimulus package and loosened monetary policies to increase bank lending while it also provided incentives to increase domestic consumption. As of 2020, the effects of COVID-19 on the Chinese economy are significantly smaller compared to the effects caused by the 2008 financial crisis. Following a deep slump at the start of the year, China's economy returned to growth in the second quarter while GDP rose 3.2 in the second quarter from a year earlier. In the third quarter of 2020 China recorded a 4.9 GDP growth.

The government is expected to offer more support on top of a raft of measures already announced, including fiscal spending boost, tax relief, and cuts in lending rates and banks' reserve requirements. Such measures have enabled China to effectively dampen the effects of the sharp decline in demand for Chinese products whereas most of the world's leading economies experienced stagnant or negative economic growth. Economists attribute much of China's rapid economic growth to two main factors: rapid productivity growth and large-scale investment, supported by foreign investment and large domestic savings. It is interesting to notice that these two factors have gone hand in hand.

The Chinese have historically maintained a high rate of savings. In fact, economic reforms led to higher efficiency in the economy, which, in return, boosted output and increased resources, which, again, led to additional investment in the economy. When reforms began in 1979, domestic savings stood at 32.5 as a percentage of GDP. However, most savings during that period were generated by the profits of state-owned enterprises (SOEs) and were used by the government for domestic investment. Economic reforms, which also included the decentralization of economic production, led to significant growth in household savings as well as corporate savings. As a consequence, China's gross savings as a percentage of GDP is the highest among leading economies. The high level of savings has enabled China to substantially increase domestic investment. Moreover, China's gross domestic savings levels far exceed its domestic investment levels, making the country a large net global lender.

Chinese real GDP growth: 1979 to 2017

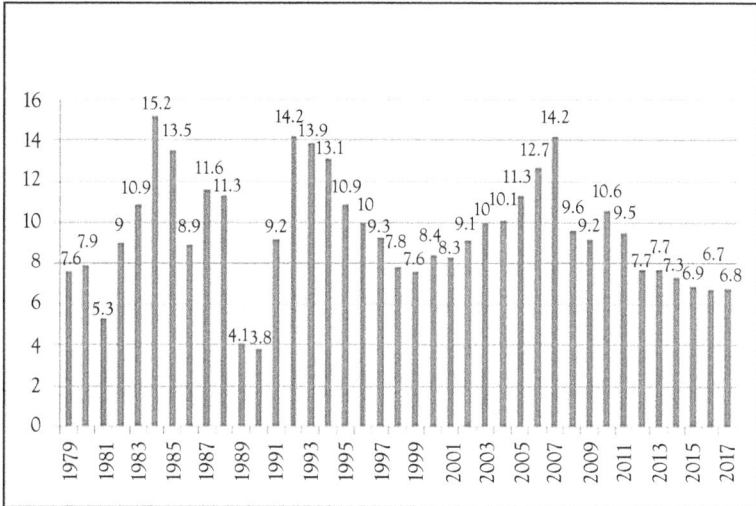

Source: Research Gate

Chinese real GDP growth: 1980 to 2019

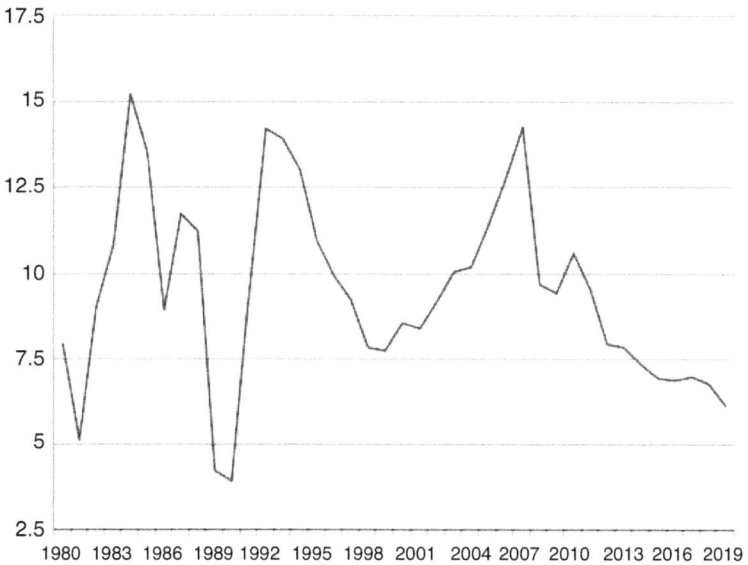

Factors Driving Consumption Growth in China from 2016 to 2021

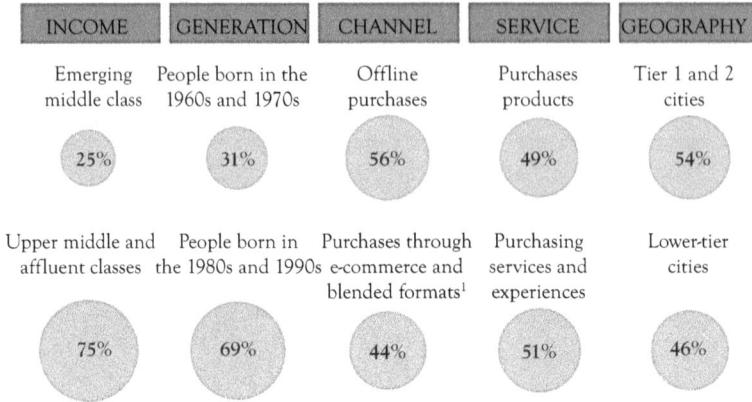

INCOME	GENERATION	CHANNEL	SERVICE	GEOGRAPHY
Emerging middle class	People born in the 1960s and 1970s	Offline purchases	Purchases products	Tier 1 and 2 cities
25%	31%	56%	49%	54%
Upper middle and affluent classes	People born in the 1980s and 1990s	Purchases through e-commerce and blended formats[1]	Purchasing services and experiences	Lower-tier cities
75%	69%	44%	51%	46%

[1]Of the contribution from e-commerce, approxiately 85% will come from mobile platforms and approximately 15% will come from PCs.

Note: This analysis breaks down the consumptio growth through 2021 into individual factors. Each column shows the contribution from a single factor, in isolation.

"Know before You Go": Devising Your China Strategy

China's market and business environment is very particular and dynamic in its essence. It welcomes all types of enterprises from different countries and with varying skills, commitment, and strategies. It can be very rewarding for many foreign businesses, especially those who conduct proper market research and craft adequate strategies to execute right from the start. China being a very diverse country with several unique market segments, it should never be seen as a single market. Even cities are divided into tier cities. While Shanghai and Beijing are considered first-tier cities, cities like Chengdu, Hangzhou, and Dalian are considered second-tier cities and a large number of small cities are considered third- and fourth-tier cities. When crafting your China strategy it is important to ensure that what you are trying to do is perceived to be in the interest of some important local political entity. If no particular government industry is excited about the project, if no Chinese partner thinks it's a good idea, then you can be sure that it is not going to be easy. It is equally important to keep in mind that for Western businesses targeting the Chinese market there are certain battles not worth fighting. My suggestion is that you avoid to compete against domestic cost-based products.

These are a few pieces of advice I believe China newcomers need to have in mind:

- Choose to fight "winnable" battles
  Some industry sectors are dominated by Chinese companies, offering competitive quality products at prices fairly lower than those most foreign companies would be able to offer. These sectors are nearly impossible for international companies to penetrate when targeting the country's mass market. In other words, there

are certain battles not worth attempting. For instance, for foreign companies seeking to compete in the consumer electronics industry, for example, washing machines, refrigerators, and air conditioners, they will find it very hard to enter because it is a volume game and winning it proves extremely difficult.

- Innovate

  A growing number of Chinese firms are becoming expert at creating products and services on par with those introduced by global companies. In this case, the best survival strategy is just to keep moving, by continually upgrading as a way to stay ahead of the domestic firms. Chinese competitors study foreign companies, their products, and how they market them. They study and learn what they do and are very good at determining what works. It is, in fact, this adaptability combined with a deep understanding of the local market that gives Chinese businesses the best of both worlds. Keep in mind that social innovation is a must. Given that domestic companies know the local culture much better than foreign businesses they can be very strong competitors. Therefore, constant innovation is a must. You need to keep moving and improving your products and services as well as your understanding of your customers' evolving needs.

- Beware of overinnovation

  One common dangerous tendency among foreign companies operating in China is to target the Chinese market by introducing higher-end products which are not only priced out of range but also include features that Chinese consumers do not need. It is essential that high-tech companies try to avoid what is called "misdirected overengineering." For instance, a few years ago, an international consumer electronics company introduced cellphone handsets built to last 10 years and phone batteries with 20-year long warranties. But who would use a cellphone for more than two years? When these products were marketed in China, local manufacturers responded by creating product versions with very similar features but sold at much lower retail prices.

- Merge, don't fight.

  As the famous saying goes "if you cannot beat them, join them." One popular—and often very effective—method of meeting the growing competition challenges coming from Chinese companies is to join forces instead of continuing to fight. A very popular strategy among many Western companies is to acquire or merge with domestic firms. In fact, for many Western companies, mergers and acquisitions offer the advantages of a JV partnership without the threats and risks that the latter might involve.

Foreign Direct Investment (FDI) Inflows and Outflows in Today's China

China now reigns as the world's largest destination for FDI, overtaking the United States for the first time in history. The nation is not only a magnet for FDI but also an important source of this type of investment. Until recently, SOEs were China's main outward investors. In fact, the first generation of Chinese multinational companies were mainly large SOEs, operating in what used to be tightly regulated, monopolized industries such as international trading, natural resources, financial services, and shipping. The second generation of large Chinese international enterprises emerged in the early to mid-1990s in very competitive manufacturing industries, especially the electronics, information, and communication technologies. Such examples include Lenovo (personal computer); Haier, TCL (consumer electronics); and Huawei Technologies and ZTE (global telecom equipment). At their inception, these firms had diverse ownership structures, including local government ownership, private ownership, or foreign participation.

Investment inflows have sped the country's move toward market capitalism, shifting the composition of the national economy away from SOEs and toward private businesses, thus welcoming the influx of foreign participation through various structures with the most popular being WFOEs and JVs. Although outward investment remains rather small in absolute terms, especially compared to the inward flow, Chinese global companies have been gaining importance as sources of international capital in recent years. The expansion of FDI into and from China has come hand in hand with a rapid economic development and an increasing openness to the rest of the world, starting with the move from restrictive to permissive policies back in the late 1970s. It was actually during the permissive period that the central government established four special economic zones in Fujian and Guangdong provinces while at the same time offering special incentive policies for FDI in these trade zones.

China's investment and trade reforms led to a surge in FDI which really began in the early 1990s. Such flows have been a great source of China's rapid economic growth and productivity gains. In 2019 foreign-invested enterprises (FIEs) in China exceeded 1 million, employing more than 100 million workers or 20 percent of the country's urban workforce. In fact, FIEs account for an important share of China's industrial output and are responsible for a significant level of China's international trade. The year 2019 saw the establishment of around 41,000 FIEs in China, with the total number of FIEs in China breaching the 1 million threshold to reach 1,001,377 in total.

A key aspect of China's growth strategy and economic modernization during the 1980s and 1990s was to attract FDI into China as a way to encourage the development of domestic companies. At that time, investment by Chinese companies overseas was sharply restricted. In 2000, however, China's leaders inaugurated a new "go global" strategy, aimed at encouraging Chinese firms to invest abroad. One major driving force of this investment is China's massive accumulation of foreign exchange reserves. FIEs currently dominate high-tech exports in China. Foreign investment in China's services industry was robust in 2019, with an increase of 12.5 percent to reach RMB 681.77 billion. Foreign investment in information technology services, information communications, and software rose by 30 percent, while for the leasing and commercial services sector the increase was almost 21 percent.

Another motivating factor behind the government's decision to encourage more FDI outflows has been to obtain natural resources—especially from Africa—such as minerals and oils, considered by the central government as necessary to sustain China's further economic growth. The Chinese government has also stated their goal of developing globally competitive Chinese firms. As China's economy continues to grow, becoming a capital-surplus economy, national policies encourage the development of domestic brands that can be considered national and global champions. In this context, acquiring foreign firms, or investing in them, is regarded as a method for Chinese firms to become more globally competitive by obtaining management skills, high-tech knowledge, as well as internationally recognized brands. As a result, a growing number of Chinese enterprises are now among the world's largest multinational corporations. Chinese firms are diversified and involved in a variety of industry sectors which, a few years ago, were state-owned, including manufacturing, banking, or natural resource exploitation. The top sources for outward FDI are mostly border and coastal provinces: Fujian, Guangdong, Heilongjiang, Jiangsu, Shandong, Shanghai, and Zhejiang. Altogether, they account for over 60 percent of China's FDI outflows. In terms of industry preference, almost 50 percent of Chinese FDI outflow is injected into the service sector, 23 percent to targeted manufacturing, 22 percent to retail and wholesale, and 17 percent is poured into the mining industry.

Since 1978, China has taken a positive yet gradual reform approach in all policy aspects related to FDI. One of the most prominent features of these reforms has been the removal of restrictions on inward FDI in the Chinese economy. It is important to note that the ideas proposed by Deng Xiaoping in 1975 to introduce and acquire advanced technology and management methods from foreign countries were further developed in the following decades to allow inward FDI into China's domestic economy. FDI was also a means of better utilizing China's resources in the absence of domestic capital back then. During the last three to four decades, China's change of attitude from restricting to encouraging inward FDI has been fully reflected by the evolution of its FDI policies.

Registered Enterprise by Business Scope

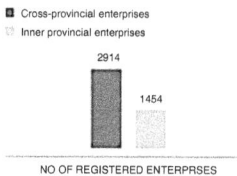

■ Cross-provincial enterprises
▨ Inner provincial enterprises

2914

1454

NO OF REGISTERED ENTERPRSES

Registered Enterprise by No. of Outlets

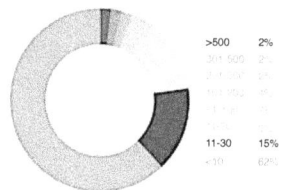

>500	2%
301-500	2%
201-300	2%
101-200	4%
31-100	7%
11-30	15%
<10	62%

Registered Enterprises by Industry

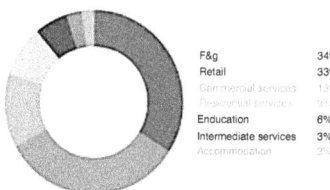

F&g	34%
Retail	33%
Commercial services	13%
Personal services	9%
Enducation	6%
Intermediate services	3%
Accommodation	2%

Registered Enterprises by Region

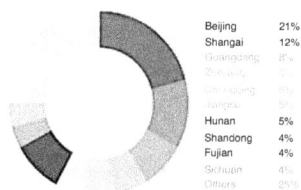

Beijing	21%
Shangai	12%
Guangdong	8%
Zhejiang	7%
Chongqing	6%
Jiangsu	6%
Hunan	5%
Shandong	4%
Fujian	4%
Sichuan	4%
Others	25%

Source: MOFCOM

FDI inflows are expected to rise marginally in 2021 due to further modest growth of the global economy.

COVID-19 and the Future of Chinese FDI

Making predictions about the economic consequences of COVID-19 for China and the world is a thankless task. The global economic activity came to a halt in the majority of countries from March 2020 onwards as part of an effort to contain the spread of the virus. Economic decline was naturally expected in the following months.

As of late 2020 many economic activities have already resumed, and while it is not yet possible to determine the scale of the damage from the drop in global demand and supply, comparing recent data on business confidence in China and the United States, two countries that have an important impact on global investment flows, might provide a hint as to the future of global investment flows to China. In the chart below, we can see that China is following a different trend compared to the United States: business confidence in China is improving toward pre-pandemic levels.

Index value

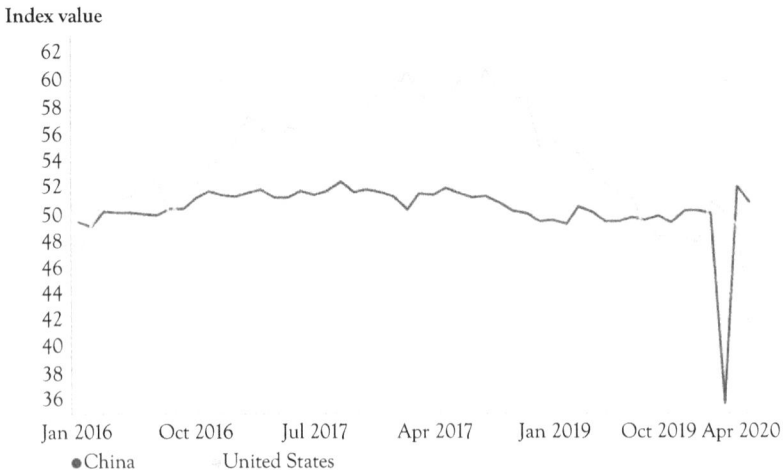

Source: UNIDO (United Nations Industrial Development Organization), 2020.
Note: The chart uses the National Bureau of Statistics Manufacturing Purchasing Manager Index for China and the ISM Manufacturing Purchasing Manager Index for the United States.

What does this mean? At the most obvious level, it means that China is resuming work and production earlier than other countries, given that business confidence in most other countries is showing trends that are similar to the United States. It is important to note that monthly production data in China confirms this trend, as we see that manufacturing output rebounded sharply in March 2020.

Manufacturing production in China

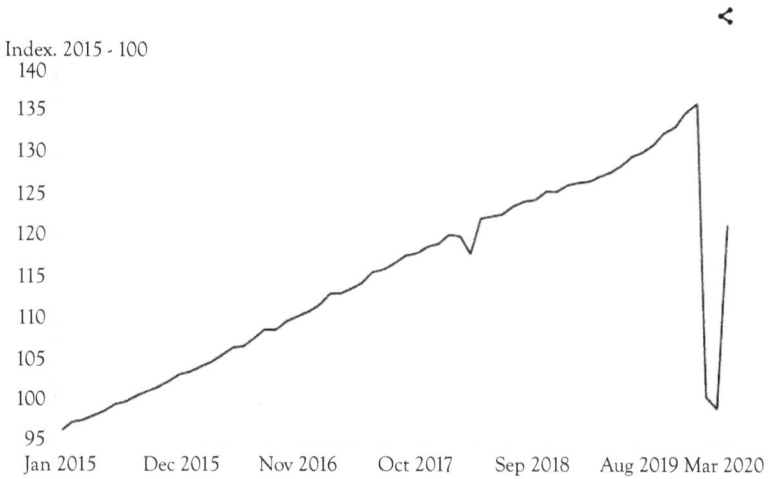

Index. 2015 - 100

Not: Seasonally adjusted.
Source: UNIDO Monthly Index of Industrial Production (IIP) database

In China, the GDP growth rate measures the change in the seasonally adjusted value of the goods and services produced by the Chinese economy. As China's traditional growth engines of manufacturing and construction are slowing down, especially after the coronavirus pandemic, services have emerged as the new driver of the Chinese economy. In the last few quarters of 2020, strength in services and local consumption helped to offset weaker manufacturing and exports.

China's GDP (2017 to 2020)

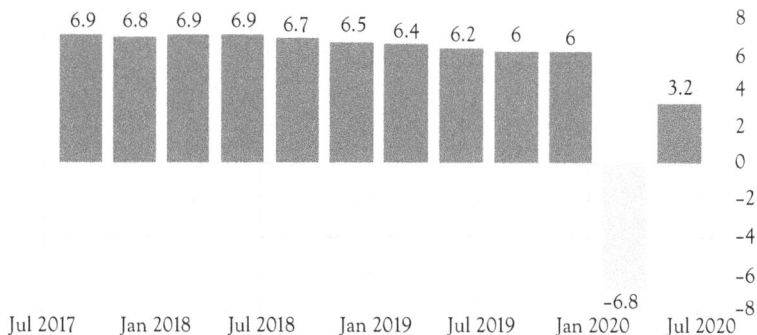

Source: China National Bureau of Statistics

China forecast: real GDP growth (2010 to 2021)

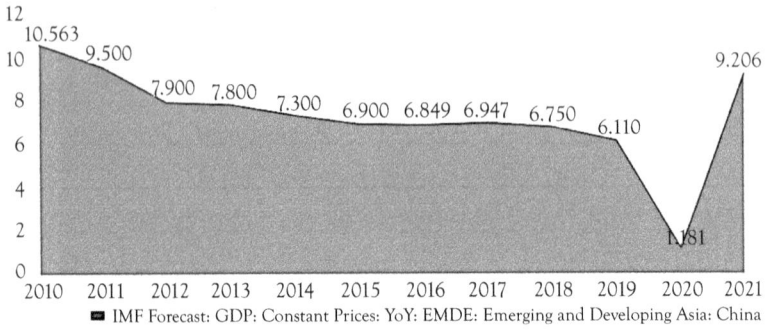

IMF Forecast: GDP: Constant Prices: YoY: EMDE: Emerging and Developing Asia: China

Source: International Monetary Fund forecast

China's Belt and Road Initiative (BRI)

China's BRI is an externally oriented development program designed to increase China's influence and investments in countries around the world and to expand international markets for Chinese products. The project aims to solidify China's global footprint and increase its economic and strategic power. BRI, formally launched in 2013, is far from being a new concept. It is rather a culmination and rebranding of previous policies and projects aimed at creating a Chinese sphere of geopolitical and economic influence. Chinese political leaders call it the "project of the century" and have included it into the nation's constitution. While BRI is the most ambitious geo-economic project in recent history, it has also been described as the "best-known, least-understood" foreign policy effort that is currently underway. China is striving to address the need for greater understanding by devoting considerable time and effort to organizing BRI events and conducting outreach. In the process, a better understanding of BRI's motives and potential has been spreading, and greater participation has naturally followed.

Broadly, BRI's land-based "belt" extends from China to Central and South Asia, to the Middle East, and then to Europe. The sea-based "road" connects China with South Asia, the Middle East, East Africa, and Europe via sea-lanes that traverse the South China Sea, Indian Ocean, Red Sea, Suez Canal, and Eastern Mediterranean. However, BRI's ambitions are not limited to just two geographic paths. Although plans for additional areas are less developed, China's vision includes Latin America, the Caribbean, the Arctic, and even outer space. By the end of January 2020, 138 countries and 30 international organizations had signed 200 Belt and Road cooperation agreements with China. The goods trade volume between China and countries involved in the initiative exceeded $6 trillion from 2013 to 2018, with an average annual growth rate of 4 percent. China has signed currency swap agreements with more than 20 countries involved in the initiative and established RMB clearing arrangements with 7 countries.

Silk Road e-commerce is becoming a new channel for economic and trade cooperation between countries. China has established the bilateral e-commerce cooperation mechanism with 17 countries.

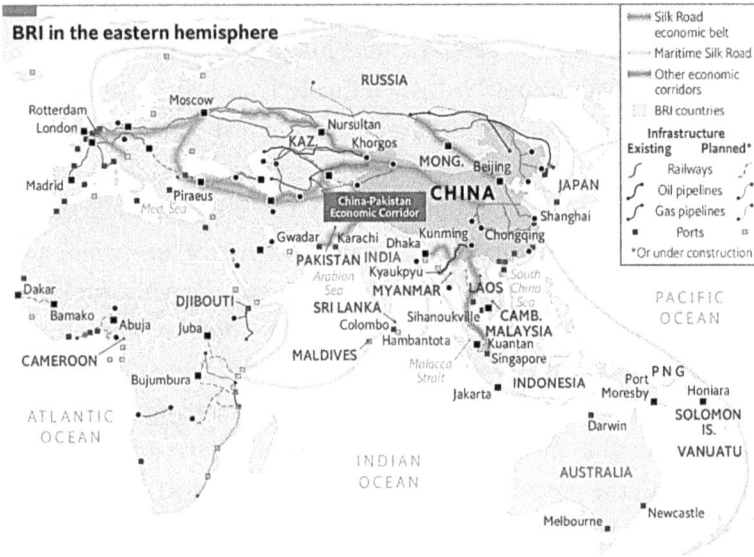

China's Belt and Road Initiative

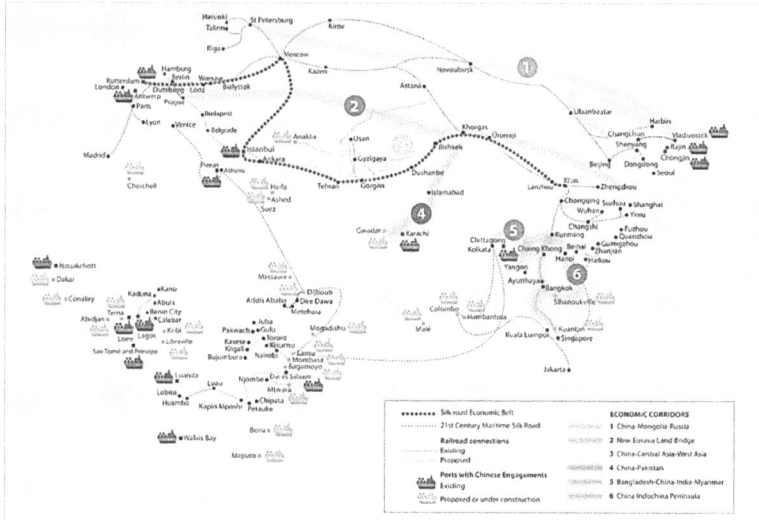

The BRI currently includes more than two-thirds of the world's countries. Extending from east to west, the BRI now encompasses as much as 65 percent of the world's population and half of global GDP. It has also come a long way from its initial conception as a massive infrastructure project connecting Asia, Europe, and Africa. A range of new international opportunities will arise as the Chinese government works to address these issues. BRI opportunities will continue to emerge in new sectors and geographies, with technology as a key area to watch as the Digital Silk Road progresses. Foreign companies being linked with Chinese suppliers through Chinese B2B platforms such as Osell and Alibaba, dubbed "matchmakers" along the Belt and Road, are expected to reap significant benefits.

So, why does the BRI matter for Western businesses? The opportunities and profit prospects will double if your company can combine their commercial activities and operations working on projects running both at home and in China. For this it is important to search opportunities the BRI presents in your home country. When first announced, investment was primarily targeted at transport infrastructure, but the whole project has steadily expanded in scope, moving into power generation, oil and gas pipelines, education, and health care, among others. BRI

Establishment of the Silk Road Fund (USD40 billion) and Asian Infrastructure Investment Bank

President Xi endorsed the Belt and Road Initiative

Belt and Road Initiative was written into the Constitution of the Communist Party of China

The number of China-Europe freight trains exceeded 12,000 in 2018

Italy became the first G7 country to sign a memorandum of understanding with China endorsing the Belt and Road Initiative

Second Belt and Road Forum for International Cooperation was held

China's Q1 trade volume with Belt and Road countries reached RMB2 trillion, growing 7.8% yoy

30+ institutions around the world co-founded the Belt and Road Economic Information Partnership

First China-Africa Economic Trade Expo was held

China proposed contruction of the Health Silk Road

Sep | 2013-15 | 2016-18 | Mar | May | 2019 | Jul | 2020 | Apr

The development of six economic coridors was proposed

The first Belt and Road Forum for International Cooperation

Trade volume between China and Belt and Road countries exceeded USD6 trillion during past five years, growing at an average annual growth rate of 4%

Luxembourg signed memorandum of understanding with China endorsing the Belt and Road initiative

Switzerland signed memorandum of understanding with China endorsing the Belt and Road initiative

China and Kazakhstan signed memorandum of understanding on cooperation plan for the connectivity of Nurla Zhol (Bright Path) new economic policy and Belt and Road initiative

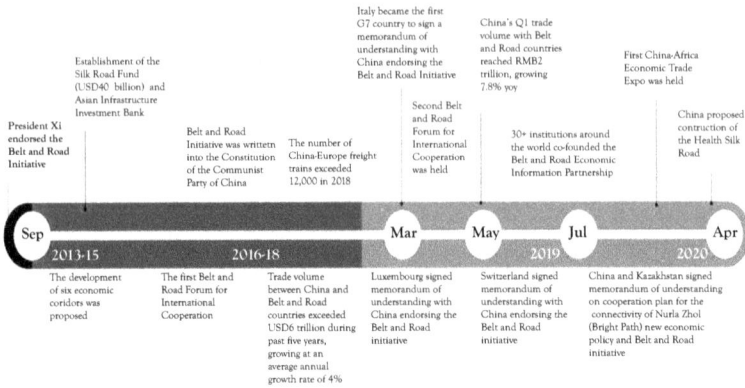

projects are typically funded in U.S. dollars, given the RMB's limited scope as a global currency. To meet this demand, China has been providing funding through its foreign reserves. However, recent years have seen the government approach the limits of its desired spending. As a result, China has begun seeking investment from international banks and investors. This will not only bring in much-needed funds, but also ensure a diversified financial participation that makes the project more resistant to geopolitical and financial risks.

Total trade volume between China and BRI countries

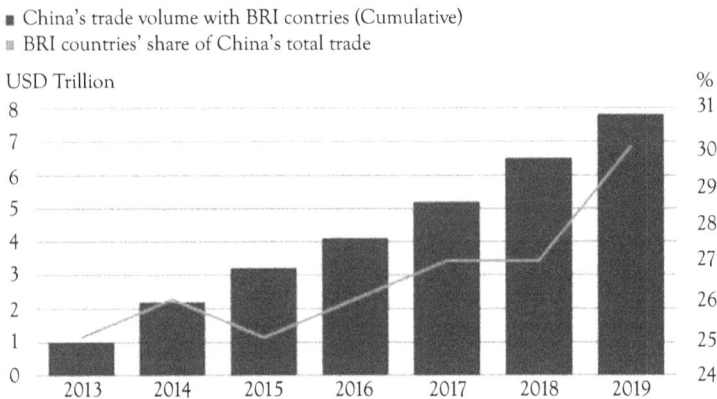

■ China's trade volume with BRI contries (Cumulative)
■ BRI countries' share of China's total trade

USD Trillion   %

	2013	2014	2015	2016	2017	2018	2019

(Bar chart values on left axis 0–8 USD Trillion, right axis 24–31 %)

Source: China's Ministry of Commerce, Belt and Road Portal, as of May 2020.

The question is what is the future of BRI in a postpandemic world? China's domestic economy contracted by 6.8 percent year-over-year in the first quarter of 2020 due to the coronavirus outbreak. While China's ability to provide ongoing funding to other countries has not suffered (foreign exchange reserves have held steady) it is expected that China will focus on domestic issues in the near term. Going forward, China may promote a wider range of financing options and more multilateral projects under the BRI umbrella. Various financing options involving multiple stakeholders in BRI projects could improve project management and decrease dependence on Chinese capital. Private financing and cofinancing had played a growing role in BRI projects, even before the pandemic, and the current situation is expected to speed this process.

Preinvestment Considerations

If you are contemplating to set up a business in China you will need to consider which structure to use. Given that strategy must always lead structure, you have to outline a strategy before deciding on a specific structure. First, you need to consider *whether* and *why* you want to invest in China, then you will need to find out *what* you should be doing before determining *how* you should proceed.

The most common motivations foreign companies choose to invest in China are:

- Market attractiveness: one that offers solid current or long-term profit potential for your business and is determined by factors such as size and growth rate of the market, cost of entry, and competition within the market.
- Consumer pull: demand exhibited by consumers, often measured as awareness, preference, and loyalty for specific brands or products.
- Operational efficiencies: several strategies and techniques used to accomplish the basic goal of delivering quality goods to customers in the most cost-effective and timely manner.

- Competitive threat: competition that hasn't occurred but has the potential to occur. In other words, it is a risk of competition.
- Stakeholder engagement: the process by which companies communicate and get to know their stakeholders. By getting to know them, companies are able to better understand what they want, when they want it, how engaged they are, and how the companies' plans and actions will affect their goals.

Although there may be various motivations at play, almost every strategy to invest in China boils down to one or more of these. Understanding which of these motivations apply in your particular case will help you reach a decision on which structure to choose. In a similar fashion, when choosing the right investment vehicle, several factors should be considered as these will lead to different tax and legal considerations. The Foreign Investment Industrial Guidance Catalogue divides industries into four main categories: encouraged, permitted, restricted, and prohibited for foreign investment. The catalogue also specifies protected industries in which foreign investment can be done only as part of a JV. Note that the high-tech, electronics, and service industries are all encouraged for foreign investments. A foreign-invested commercial enterprise (FICE), which can be set up either as a WOFE or as a JV, is a type of company for franchising, retailing, or distribution operations. Additionally, a WOFE or a JV can be established exclusively as a FICE or can combine FICE activities with other business activities such as services and manufacturing.

Broad Methods of Market Entry

Since China's entry into the WTO back in 2001, the Chinese government has continued to fulfill its WTO engagements by gradually opening up various sectors to foreign investors. Along these lines, the government's stated goal is to further improve the foreign investment structure especially by encouraging foreign investment in the high-end manufacturing industry as well as the strategic and modern service industries with subsidies, administrative convenience, as well as tax and tariff incentives. Despite the current tumultuous global financial environment, recent data published by MOFCOM, the Chinese Ministry of Commerce, shows that China is continuing to attract impressive amounts of FDI. Foreign investment into China comes in several foreign-invested entity forms. Choosing the appropriate structure depends on a number of factors, including business scope, industry sector, and investment size.

Despite certain challenges, China is a great place for many companies. Foreign companies have the possibility to manufacture in China, to sell into China, or to source their goods from China. Exporting your products is one way to enter the Chinese market and it is the least risky one, in terms of both operational cost and invested capital. While each mode of entry presents its strengths and weaknesses, the great majority of companies usually prefer to develop a gradual approach based on their available resources and time. When deciding which method of entry is the most suitable for your business it is necessary to consider the size of your company, the time and resources available, the nature of the products or services you want to sell, the business conditions and regulations applying to the particular industry your products belong to, and whether there is need for on-the-ground representation (e.g., marketing and after-sales service).

The export of products to China involves engagement of a company which has an import–export license in accordance with Chinese laws. Therefore, such a company must be registered in China, in which case the term "importer" in Chinese trade terminology refers to China-based companies possessing an import–export license. Although exporting generally requires considerable time investment, it is a good option for companies that want to avoid the costs of setting up in China but are still attracted by the profit potential of the Chinese market. From a practical perspective, direct export is suitable for services or technology or for unique products of smaller quantities where an established distribution network is not necessary. Another major advantage is the cutting out of middlemen such as agents and other intermediaries.

The downside is that such companies will have to be responsible for conducting their own market research as well as carrying out all the required administrative procedures such as ensuring that their products, services, or technology can enter the Chinese market and that relevant standards and licensing and labeling requirements are met. Additionally,

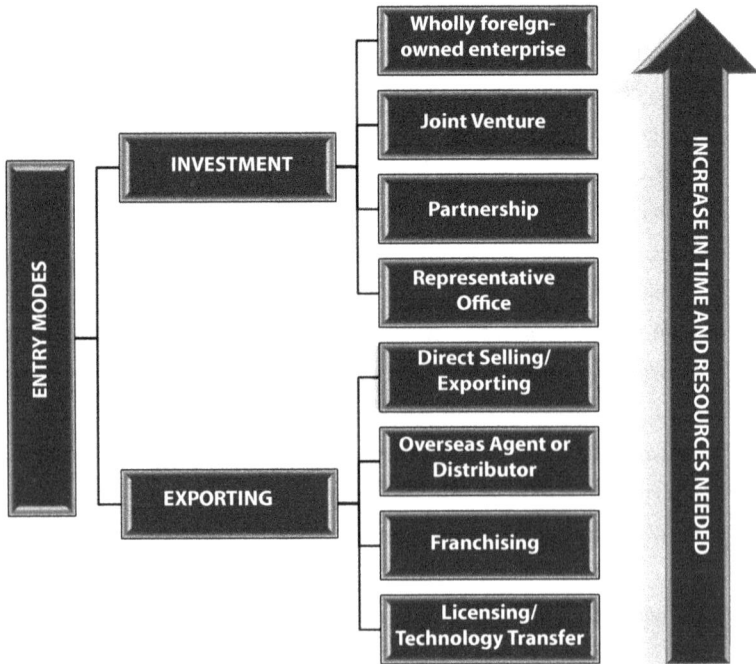

companies will have to handle relations with financial institutions, freight forwarders, and customs procedures if those are not handled by a Chinese importer. It might be very time consuming at the early stages but in the long run the result will be that companies will develop a much deeper understanding of the Chinese market, their customers, and the processes of trading in China. To find out more about exporting strategies to China available to Western businesses, you may refer to the book *Trading with China: Exporting Goods, Services and Technology to the Chinese Market.*

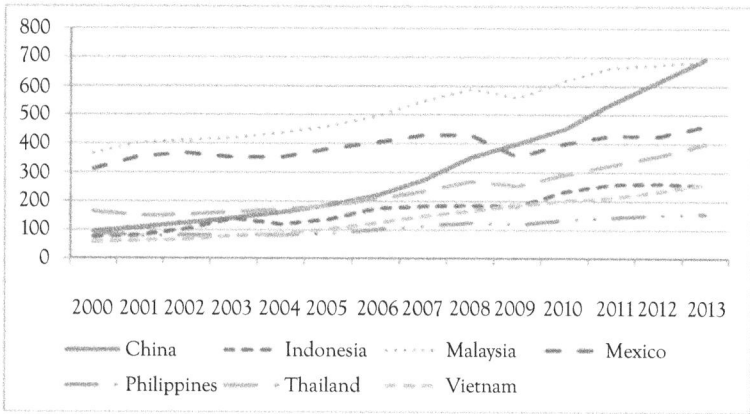

Market Opportunities and Challenges

As already mentioned, China's huge population and low wage rates gave it a significant competitive advantage when economic reforms and trade liberalization first began. This advantage, however, appears to be eroding as wages in China have risen significantly in the last years. For instance, from 2000 to 2020 Chinese average wages grew at an average annual rate of 11.4 percent. As you can see in the given figure, China's average monthly wages were RMB 7,000 in 2010 compared with $311 for Mexico in the same year (meaning that Chinese wages were 30.2 percent the size of Mexican monthly wages). In 2013, however, Chinese monthly wages averaged $1,000 and were 45.5 percent higher than the Mexican wages, which averaged $461. When compared to Vietnam, the gap is even bigger. In 2000, Chinese average wages were 92 percent higher than the

Minimum wages in developing countries from approximately 2010 to 2019

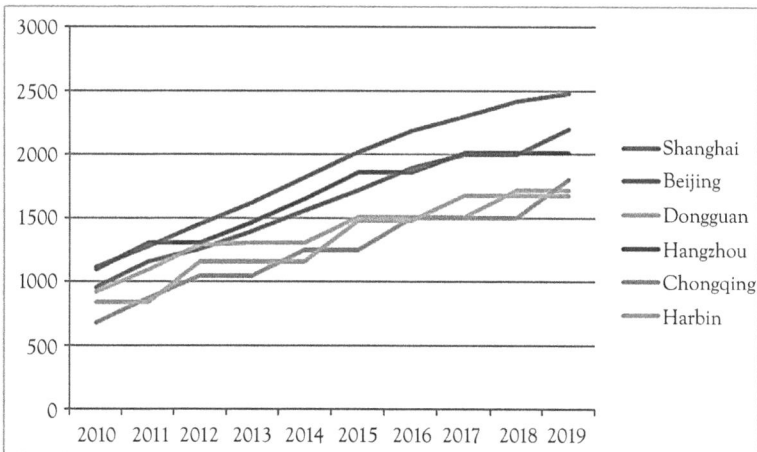

Source: MOFCOM, IMF

Labor costs across the world

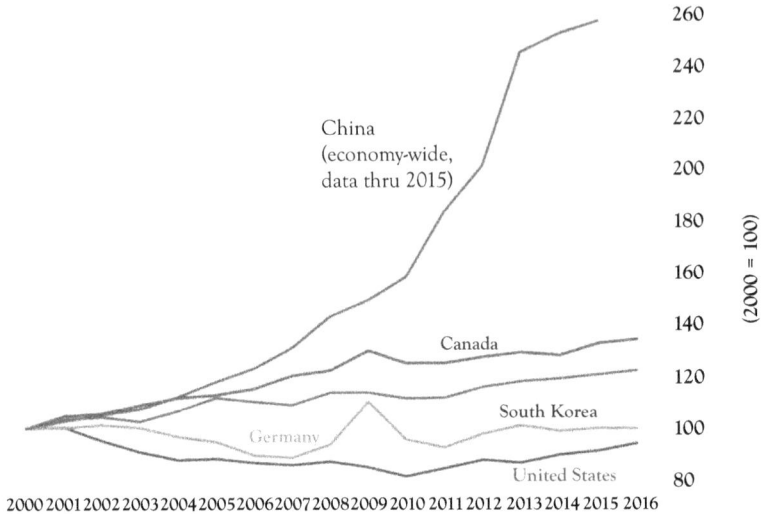

Source: MOFCOM, IMF

ones in Vietnam, whereas in 2013 they were 168 percent higher. In late 2018, in a survey conducted by the American Chamber of Commerce of its member companies in China, 60 percent of respondents reported that rising labor costs ranked as the biggest business risk facing their China operations. Rising labor costs are also one of the main reasons why the Chinese government decided to focus on boosting innovation, domestic consumption, and productivity levels as main drivers of growth.

China's 13th Five-Year Plan (FYP) 2016 to 2020

China's FYPs are a series of five-year national development agendas focused on social and economic development. The first FYP was issued in 1953 during the regime of Chairman Mao Zedong and was influenced by the FYPs of the Soviet Union. For nearly seven decades, the FYPs have been the vehicles by which the Chinese government instituted reforms and shaped the economy of China. They provide goals and direction toward the long-term development of the country. The purpose of FYPs is to help the government and civilians to be "on the same page" regarding the importance and purpose of public initiatives. By announcing the country's main strategic goals to the people, the party strives to give a sense of direction and unity to the country. For foreign expatriates and businesses, understanding the plan may give important insights into future policies that may significantly impact the business environment of China in years to come. There is also a very tangible and practical aspect to China's FYPs. In facing the sudden outbreak of COVID-19, China made swift and decisive decisions to deal with the pandemic and avoided turning this public health issue into an economic and social crisis.

China had stated ambitious goals of restructuring the economy in the period from 2016 to 2020. China's 13th FYP is the key catalyst for this change. This document is not only a strong indicator of the direction of the economy, but also a signpost for opportunities offered to Western entrepreneurs and SMEs. The key themes emerging from the current plan are economic restructuring, promotion of social equality, and protection of the environment. Western companies that can match government policy initiatives are likely to be more successful in getting investment approvals, benefitting from supporting policies (e.g., tax breaks) winning public procurement bids, being able to register their products or services on preferential catalogues, as well as finding buyers for their products. In fact, seven industries have been highlighted in the 13th FYP as major areas for the future growth and prosperity of China. Plans regarding these industries are aimed at moving beyond mere low-end manufacturing toward the development of global brands and services marking China as a 21st century innovative production leader.

The industries you can see below offer significant opportunities to Western businesses. In future, the Chinese government will invest heavily in these areas and will also provide important tax, fiscal, and procurement incentives for those companies seeking to operate within these sectors in China. While China's ultimate objective is to develop strong national and international players, Western companies having a technological advantage and know-how in areas where China is still weak will find eager local partners and opportunities not to be missed.

China's 13th Five-Year Plan (2016 to 2020)

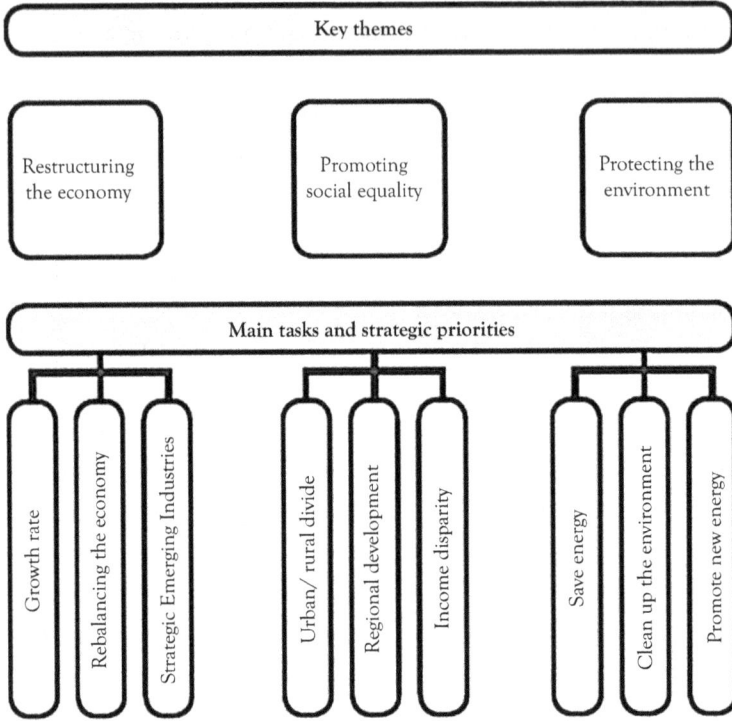

Key themes

| Restructuring the economy | Promoting social equality | Protecting the environment |

Main tasks and strategic priorities

- Growth rate
- Rebalancing the economy
- Strategic Emerging Industries
- Urban/ rural divide
- Regional development
- Income disparity
- Save energy
- Clean up the environment
- Promote new energy

The 10 general themes of this most recent plan are as follows:

1. Roll out with more stringent enforcement.
2. Stimulate innovation and technological growth.
3. Control outbound investments.
4. Focus strongly on carbon footprint and projected image.
5. Invest in infrastructure.
6. Ensure the growth of income per capita.
7. Invest in senior care to promote a longer average life expectancy.
8. Stimulate local and international education.
9. Realize more Internet growth.
10. Realize stable economic growth.

Encompassing these themes, the aspirations of this FYP are two-fold. First, through innovation, China strives to become a qualitative production leader through innovation-driven technology developments. Second, China seeks to continue developing a circular economy, where market forces will become the main driving force behind sustainable product development and recycling. By promoting a circular economy, China hopes to advance its environmental technology, ecology, and culture.

China's 14th Five-Year Plan (2021 to 2025)

As early as September 2019, Xi Jinping mentioned the drafting of the 14th FYP in a meeting on national harmony. In December of the same year, during an economic meeting, he stressed the importance of economic planning for the 14th FYP. Given the growing uncertainties resulting from the effects of the coronavirus pandemic on the global economy in 2020, the 14th FYP has attracted great attention. Against the backdrop of increasingly strained China–U.S. ties and an external environment characterized by rising protectionism and a global economic downturn, China has sent the goal to boost its economy by relying on its massive consumer market as a way to cope with fast-evolving external risks. It is expected that a development pattern centered on "internal circulation," supplemented by the "external circulation," would be set by the 14th FYP. While the 14th FYP is still on the making, there are four current policy trends in China that are likely to give direction to the research and planning phases of the 14th FYP. These are the following:

- Incentivizing the research of artificial intelligence technology
- Prioritizing the development of 5G technology
- Supporting initiatives to build up less-developed areas
- Continuous push for green development

These trends will most likely continue to promote the development of the *robotics industry* and the *circular economy* in China.

Robotics Industry

Main societal drivers such as rising labor costs, shortage of skilled staff, and the aging society have contributed to the Chinese government's increased focus on the robotics industry. Previously, China had announced goals to increase its domestic robotics industry to 50 percent of the global market share, has 100,000 domestic robots in operation, and aims to have 150 robots per 10,000 employees by the year 2020. Furthermore, by 2025, it aims to have 70 percent of the domestic market internally produced and 1.8 million industrially functioning units.

These ambitions are likely to manifest strongly in China's upcoming FYP. The main sectors that use industrial robots, such as the car industry, continue to grow at rates which have exceeded previous forecasts. Because of this, there is a greater demand for industrial robots. At the same time, the Chinese middle class is growing. This growth provides an expanding market to service robots such as health care devices and catering robots. In 2016, foreign manufacturers comprised 67.10 percent of this industry, with the main players being Fanuc, Kuka, ABB, and Yaskawa. The absence of certain robotics technology in China gives the Western world the opportunity to bring their know-how in the coming years.

Circular Economy

Recycling is another area where the next FYP may strongly emphasize. The Chinese e-commerce industry holds half of the global market share. It accounts for 70 percent of packaging materials in China. The gross merchandise volume of this industry has grown from less than 1 trillion RMB in 2011 to around 9 trillion RMB at the end of 2018. Unsurprisingly, the volume of parcels has 10-folded in this same time period. Yet 90 percent of plastic parcel packaging wastes are not recycled.

Consequently, the Chinese government has been consistently pushing for a "circular economy" as early as 2006. Chinese government has built the foundation for the growth and development of the recycling industry through ambitious initiatives incentivizing companies. By 2020, China aims to increase the recycling rate of large wastes to approximately 55 percent. Moreover, it aims to institute recycling reforms in 75 percent of national industrial parks and 50 percent of provincial industrial parks. Challenges hindering the development of the circular economy in China give foreign industry pioneers the opportunity to bring in their skills and expertise.

Why Are China's Five-Year Plans Significant to Businesses?

Although the 14th FYP has yet to be formulated, properly forecasting what it may entail will allow businesses to better mitigate risks and exploit the opportunities of tomorrow. FYPs give an indication in which direction the Chinese government will move, and businesses can learn and adapt their business to align to this direction. A good illustration of this principle is the example of how the recent FYPs supported the growth of the circuit chip industry in China. In June 2011, the integrated circuit industry was included as part of the high-technology sector of the Chinese economy that is given priority for development. In March 2015, the government passed favorable tax policies for chip manufacturing enterprises to support this industry. A year later, China further amended these policies by providing even greater tax incentives. Manufacturing enterprises that have proven themselves especially successful through continual improvement and innovation became eligible for additional tax reduction. Furthermore, in April 2018, a legislation strengthening the promotion and application of common military and civilian standards opened new market opportunities for these integrated circuit companies.

Key Industry Opportunities for Foreign Businesses

Sustainable Development: After decades of environmental degradation, China has been increasingly focusing on technologically advanced and environmentally friendly goods and services. Many Western businesses are in possession of know-how and technologies which are able to help China to ensure that its future development will be sustainable.

Consumption: Another major focus of the government is to encourage domestic consumption. The government has set the aim to increase the corresponding share of the GDP to 50 percent by 2030, by lowering taxes, creating free-trade zones, raising minimum wages by 13 percent every year, and implementing policies aimed at boosting consumer confidence and access to credit. Many Western products are already benefitting from these policies. For instance, European luxury brands are doing extremely well in the Chinese market. China's retail sector, although fiercely competitive, is widely open.

Social Issues: The country is currently facing many social challenges, including the need for health care reforms, access to education, social security funding, environmental problems, and food safety. As China continues to face growing disparities between the rich and the poor, urban and rural areas, western and eastern regions, government attention, reforms, and spending are all expected to increase in the coming years.

Trade and Currency Issues: After facing strong global pressure regarding its "undervalued currency," China successfully decreased its account surplus. Although this is not an opportunity per se, it does impact foreign businesses in China. In fact, appreciation of the Chinese RMB is a mixed blessing. On the one hand, it benefits Western exporters to China by making their goods cheaper and thus more affordable to Chinese consumers. On the other hand, it makes goods produced in China more costly to export out of China. Domestic and foreign companies importing and exporting goods can be heavily affected by exchange rate volatility and perhaps, they will need to consider hedging against this type of risks.

Demographics: China being the most populated country in the world, Western company should conduct their market research in a way that allows them to make the most out of the emerging opportunities created

China takes the lead on renewables

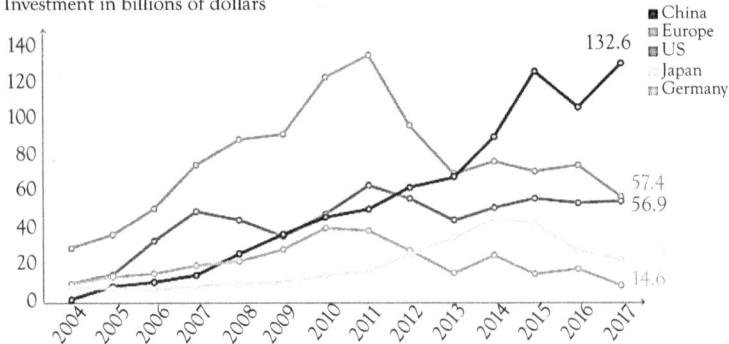

by changing demographics. As an example, the number of elderly people compared to the younger population—commonly known as "dependency ratio"—continues to rise. As a result, there is a growing demand for
decent health care services. According to predictions by the World Bank,
China's dependency ratio will reach 34.4 percent in the rural regions of
the country by 2030.

Ten key investment fields in the 13th five-year plan

CHINA'S TECHNOLOGICAL REVOLUTION

GROWTH ACHIEVED

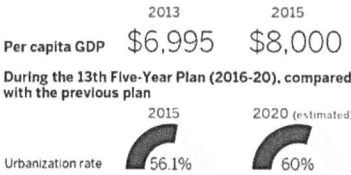

	2013	2015
Per capita GDP	$6,995	$8,000

During the 13th Five-Year Plan (2016-20), compared with the previous plan

	2015	2020 (estimated)
Urbanization rate	56.1%	60%

Volume of foreign direct investment Unit: $ billion

116.01 (2011), 111.72 (2012), 117.59 (2013), 119.56 (2014), 126.27 (2015)

INTERNET PLUS AND 5G TELECOM TECHNOLOGY

Online retail spending Unit: $ billion — 442.2 to 1,132.8 ('14–'20e)

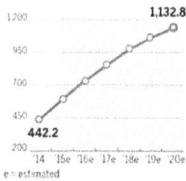

Online buyers Unit: million — 362.6 to 639.1

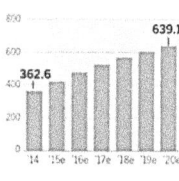

Number of Internet users and mobile Internet users Unit: million
Internet users: 513, 564, 618, 649, 688
Mobile Internet users: 355.6, 420, 500.1, 556.8, 619.8

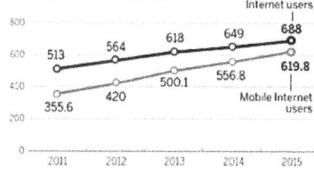

Internet penetration rate Unit: %
38.3% (2011), 42.1% (2012), 45.8% (2013), 47.9% (2014), 50.3% (2015), 70% (2020e)

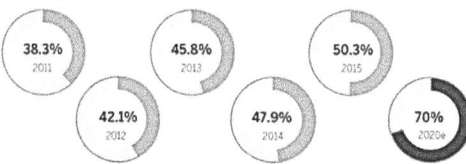

Proportion of Chinese companies conducting online marketing campaigns Unit: %
24.2% to 33.8%

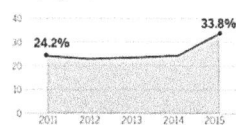

Number of websites Unit: million
2015: 4.23, 2014: 3.35, 2013: 3.20, 2012: 2.68, 2011: 2.30

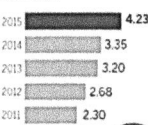

MEDICAL INDUSTRY Output value Unit: trillion yuan
10 (2020e), 2.88 (2015), 2.58 (2014), 2.23 (2013), 1.88 (2012), 1.56 (2011)

Ten key investment fields in the 13th Five-Year Plan: Agricultural modernization; Infrastructure investment; Internet Plus and 5G telecom technology; Environmental protection and eco-friendly goods; Reform of State-owned enterprises; Belt and Road Initiative; Building world-class city clusters in the Beijing-Tianjin-Hebei region; Healthcare and retirement; Clean-energy autos; Intelligent manufacturing

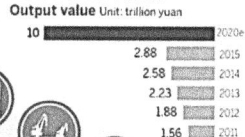

Source: The China Internet Network Information Center, The National Bureau of Statistics

Industry Applications

I cannot stress enough how important it is to determine straight from the beginning the official status of the industry sector your business falls into and, hence, whether or not some form of Chinese involvement will be needed. To find out, you should refer to the so-called "Catalogues," which are two different documents. The first is the Catalogue for the Guidance of Foreign Investment Industries, applying to the whole of China, and the second is the Catalogue of Priority Industries for Foreign Investment and covers the Central-Western Region. The Catalogue for the Guidance of Foreign Investment, published by the National Development and Reform Commission (NDRC) and the Ministry of Commerce (MOFCOM), categorizes industries as encouraged, permitted, restricted, and prohibited to foreign investment.

Permitted and Encouraged Industries

Permitted: This category includes a wide range of sectors. Any industry not listed in the other categories is "permitted."

Encouraged: These include sectors that promote the development of agriculture and high technology, upgrade product quality, promote environmental protection, and promote exports, which help the growth of the poorer and less-developed inland regions. These industry sectors enjoy special incentives.

Restricted and Prohibited Industries

Restricted: This category includes environmentally unfriendly, technologically backward industries or industries opened to foreign investment on a pilot basis.

Prohibited: These industries are those using technology unique to China, those harming the country's national interests and ethics, or those that are damaging to human health and the environment.

EO Intelligence: Stage of Major Technologies in 2019

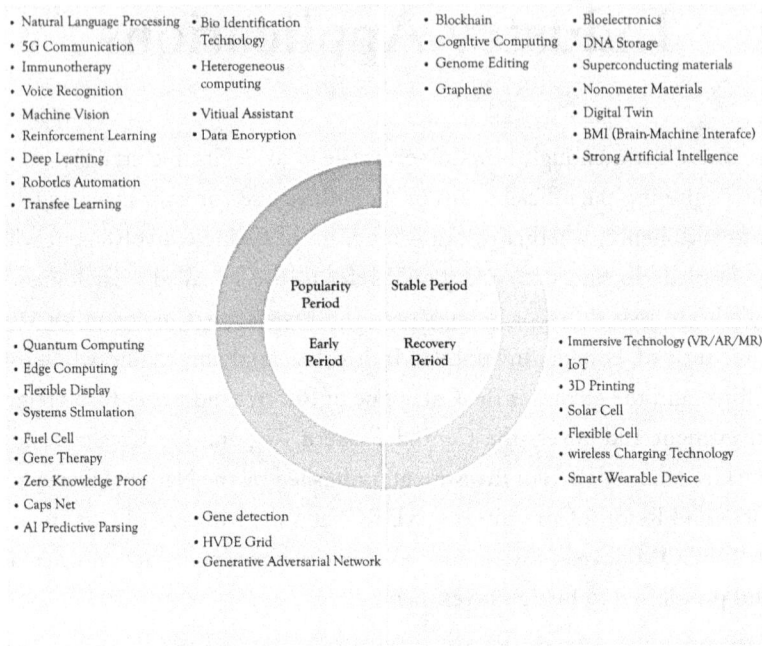

- Natural Language Processing
- 5G Communication
- Immunotherapy
- Voice Recognition
- Machine Vision
- Reinforcement Learning
- Deep Learning
- Robotics Automation
- Transfee Learning

- Bio Identification Technology
- Heterogeneous computing
- Vitiual Assistant
- Data Enoryption

- Blockhain
- Cognltive Computing
- Genome Editing
- Graphene

- Bioelectronics
- DNA Storage
- Superconducting materials
- Nonometer Materials
- Digital Twin
- BMI (Brain-Machine Interafce)
- Strong Artificial Intellgence

Popularity Period   Stable Period

- Quantum Computing
- Edge Computing
- Flexible Display
- Systems Stlmulation
- Fuel Cell
- Gene Therapy
- Zero Knowledge Proof
- Caps Net
- AI Predictive Parsing

Early Period   Recovery Period

- Immersive Technology (VR/AR/MR)
- IoT
- 3D Printing
- Solar Cell
- Flexible Cell
- wireless Charging Technology
- Smart Wearable Device

- Gene detection
- HVDE Grid
- Generative Adversarial Network

Certain industries, especially those falling into the "encouraged" and "restricted" categories, are exclusively open to Sino-foreign JV enterprises or entities with a limited percentage of foreign investment. The most recent version of the Catalogue added more environmentally friendly and high-end projects to the "encouraged" category, including new, environmental-friendly materials, automotive parts and components resulting in energy savings, environmental-friendly battery manufacturing technology, creation of water recycling facilities, and investment in charging facilities for electric vehicles. In the encouraged category were also included aerospace, aviation, light motorcycles, advanced semiconductor development, advanced generation equipment for Internet and network systems, and exploration and exploitation of unconventional natural gas resources. The recent version of the Catalogue reflects China's aim to further restrict projects requiring heavy energy consumption or those projects causing high levels of pollution as well as the desire to impose stricter controls in the housing bubbles, by prohibiting foreign investment in the construction of luxury residencies and villas.

The latest version of the Catalogue of Priority Industries for Foreign Investment in the Central-Western Region contains a total of 411 so-called "priority industries" in 21 provinces and autonomous regions in the Central and Western regions. Unlike the Catalogue for the Guidance of Foreign Investment Industries, it contains only priority industries and all projects listed in the catalogue benefit from preferential policies such as the ability to obtain custom duty exemptions. The lion's share of FDI currently remains in the manufacturing industry while significant amounts are starting to move into services and the tertiary and the primary sector as an increasing number of areas are opened up and the Chinese economy grows more sophisticated.

Apart from a few sectors considered harmful to national interests and national security, most products or services fall within the freely importable goods category. Agriculture, food manufacturing, textile, processing of petroleum and nuclear fuel, manufacture of raw chemical products and materials, nonmetallic mineral products, general and special purpose machinery, transport equipment, production of electric and heat power, and environmental management industry to name just a few belong in the "restricted" category.

Tightly Regulated Industries and Their Respective Approval Bodies

Industry	Approval authority
Manufacturing and trading	MOFCOM (Ministry Of Commerce) or its designated local authority
Telecommunications and IT	MMI (Ministry of Information Industries) or its designated local authority
Banking and finance	PBOC (People's Bank of China)
Insurance	CIRC (China Insurance Regulatory Commission)
Legal	MOJ (Ministry of Justice)
Accounting	MOF (Ministry of Finance)
Airlines	MCA (Ministry of Civil Aviation)
Media and entertainment	MOC (Ministry of Culture)

It is important to be aware whether your intended activities fall into the "encouraged" sector. If so, your company may apply for substantial benefits in the reduction of tax rates. On the other hand, if you are not aware of these advantages your business stands to miss out a lot in terms of saved revenues. As with all business applications, encouraged status applications need to go through MOFCOM or its local office for approval and they are approved by the National Development and Reform Commission.

It is worth noting that, as it is common practice in China, officials appear to apply some administrative discretion to the definitions with different categories. For instance, we have been able to negotiate cases where a manufacturing company wished to manufacture product A which did not fall in the "encouraged" category. However, product B, a by-product of their process, fell within the "encouraged" category. We finally managed to frame their business scope not around product A but product B and hence obtained the "encouraged" industry status.

If a WFOE wishes to apply to be evaluated as "encouraged sector" after it has been established, such as in the case with the modification or addition to its business scope, or in the event this had been previously overlooked, the company must submit the following documents to the relevant authorities: application form, copy of the business license, feasibility report, certificate of approval, list of imported machinery and equipment with detailed description of number, unit, and total price. In case the application involves an increase of capital, the company must also submit an audit report to the original approval authority.

Before making any step toward setting up an entity in China you need to conduct a thorough search and study carefully the applicable legislation. Next you will find a list of all applicable legislation documents that you need to search before making any steps toward creating an entity in China:

Applicable Legislation

- Catalogue for the Guidance of Foreign Investment Industries
- Catalogue of Advantageous Sectors for Foreign Investment in Central and Western Regions

- Law on Chinese-Foreign Equity Joint Ventures
- Law on Chinese-Foreign Contractual Joint Ventures and its Implementation Regulations
- Law on Wholly Foreign-Owned Enterprise and its Implementation
- Regulation on Administration of Commercial Franchise
- Administrative Measures on Establishment of Partnership Enterprises by Foreign Enterprises or Individuals
- The Company Law of the People's Republic of China
- Law of the People's Republic of China on Enterprises Operated Exclusively with Foreign Capital
- PRC Corporate Income Tax Law
- The Catalogue of Import-Export Commodities Subject to Compulsory Inspection and Quarantine
- Measures for the Administration of Prohibited and Restricted Import of Technologies
- Foreign Exchange Control Regulations of the People's Republic of China
- Catalogue of Technologies Prohibited and Restricted from Import

Types of Companies with Easier Access to China

While great achievements have been made to attract and encourage foreign investments through various reforms, some business activities are still hardly accessible to foreigners. To minimize burdens and red tape when establishing a legal presence in China I recommend these four encouraged business structures which generally secure easier access to China.

Consulting Services Company

Given the increasing demand for professional consulting services (e.g., education, management, insurance, accounting, or tourism), consulting services companies are among the most encouraged forms of business in China. Establishing a consultancy firm is easy and the process is simple mainly because of the low requirement for capital. Many leading Western consulting firms have opened WOFEs in China and offer consulting services.

Trading Company

Trading companies, commonly referred to as FICEs, currently present tremendous opportunities in China. For instance, as the country is committed to WTO a variety of new regulations have been set up to liberalize the distribution and retail sector for foreign companies trading in China. Foreign trading companies are allowed to engage in the following business activities:

- Retail company involving the sale of products/merchandise for personal or household consumption either from a China-based fixed location or away from a fixed location
- Wholesale company involving the sale of products/ merchandise to retailers or to industrial, commercial, institutional, and other business professionals, or to other wholesalers and related subordinated services

Manufacturing Company

China has long been known as the world's factory. The local government has encouraged the creation of manufacturing companies by offering advantages of low labor costs, tax incentives, and excellent infrastructure such as transportation and innovative technology. As a result, many foreign companies moved their production lines to China. Many local governments have created industrial zones providing tax and other incentives to attract foreign investors to set up manufacturing companies in their cities. It is important that you search and compare the available options to find the best fit according to your company's specific needs.

On the other hand, certain types of manufacturing activities such as book publishing, automobiles, medicines, salt, pesticides, agricultural chemicals, petroleum, and crude oil are still controlled by the Chinese government. Foreign investors are not completely prohibited from entering these industries but regulations and restrictions enacted by the government to exert control over the supply and demand of these goods make the whole process extremely cumbersome and time consuming. All manufacturing companies are required to apply for various licenses or approvals with local bureaus and authorities. It is important to note that the registration process for this type of companies is generally more complicated than the one you would normally follow to set up a consulting company due to the fact that manufacturing plants usually require additional certifications such as a rather big number of reports as well as environment evaluation certifications. When it comes to the incorporation of manufacturing companies the minimum required registered capital varies among industries.

High-Tech Enterprise

Currently, the demands of the local high-tech industry for more sophisticated high-tech components such as software, research and development centers, or technology are more pressing in China. Chinese local companies, especially businesses, are expected to enhance their ability in sectors such as research and development and learning technology through cooperation with foreign high-tech companies. The Chinese government has formulated several policies favorable to foreign investment in order to encourage strategic alliances between local businesses and foreign enterprises. Apart from making great efforts to promote the development of the country's high-tech industry, both domestically and internationally, the Chinese government imposed strict policies for the protection of the IPR of high-tech products for wholly owned foreign high-tech enterprises in China. An increasing number of local governments have set up High-Tech Zones where they provide tax and other advantages to attract foreign investors. In 2020 China's High-Tech Zones maintained growth despite the impact of the COVID-19 epidemic. In May 2020, the revenue of these zones reached ¥3.27 trillion, up 10.3 than the previous year.

China has emerged as one of the most aggressive countries promoting 5G technology. It is predicted to become one of the top three markets driving the growth of 5G in Asia and is projected to become the world's largest 5G market by 2025. The Chinese government's Belt and Road techno-nationalist policy has set the goal to reduce the country's dependence on foreign technology and achieve global technological leadership.

China's Digital 'Belt and Road'

Chinese companies are expanding their global footprint, installing fiber-optic cable, surveillance systems, and telecommunications equipment in dozens of countries around the world.

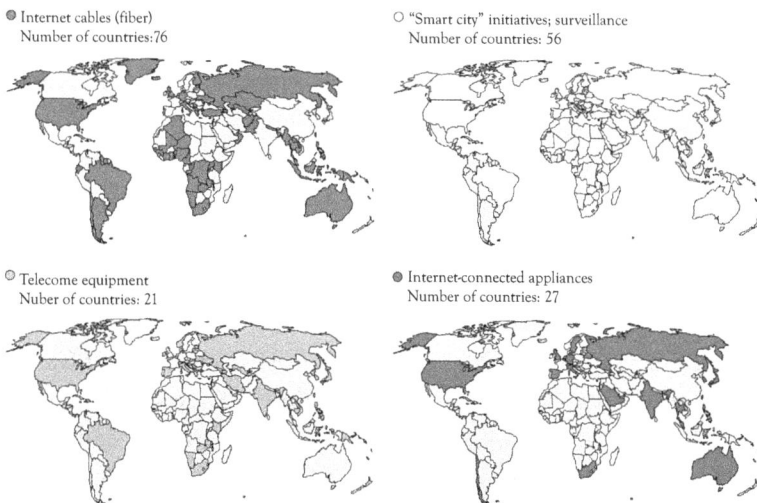

● Internet cables (fiber)
Number of countries: 76

○ "Smart city" initiatives; surveillance
Number of countries: 56

◎ Telecome equipment
Nuber of countries: 21

● Internet-connected appliances
Number of countries: 27

Expanding network
China's spending on Digital Silk Road projects, by country

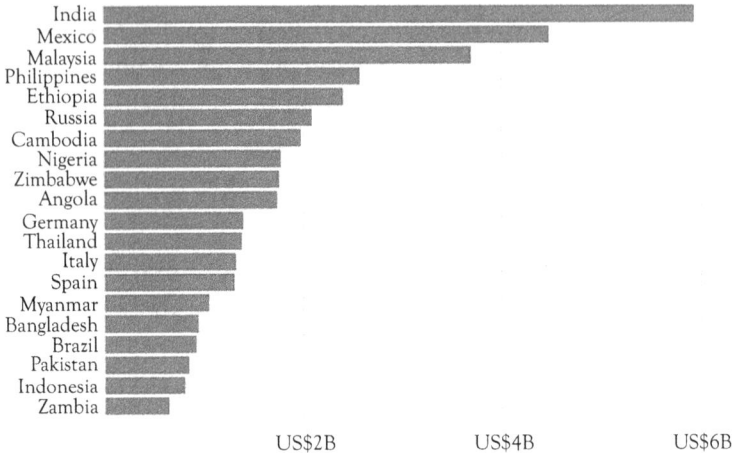

Source: MOFCOM, China's National Bureau of Statistics

The BRI, dubbed the "Digital Silk Road," currently amounts to an estimated U.S.$79 billion worth of projects around the world, covering optical fiber cables, 5G networks, satellites, and devices that connect to these systems. The Digital Silk Road is estimated to require a total investment of U.S.$200 billion. China's president, Xi Jinping, the architect of BRI, has announced that the Digital Silk Road will also encompass quantum computing, nanotechnology, artificial intelligence, big data, and cloud storage, that is, all areas in which China is on track to become the world's leading innovator and filer of patents. Chen Zhaoxiong, China's vice-minister of Information Technology, recently stated that China intends to create "*a community of common destiny in cyberspace.*"

The most tangible infrastructural components of the Digital Silk Road encompass two major undertakings. The first is the upgrading of Internet connections across the Belt and Road regions in the form of new undersea cables linking east and west and rolling out broadband in dozens of countries where such infrastructure is either underdeveloped or nonexistent. The second component of this project is a massive expansion of China's BeiDou navigation satellite network to rival the U.S.-owned global positioning system. Some U.S.$25 billion will be spent on expanding the BeiDou network from 17 satellites covering the Far East to 35 covering the entire world. The new satellites were launched in 2018 and the system was completed in early 2020.

Official documents from the BeiDou system office state that China plans to establish a "ubiquitous, integrated and intelligent, comprehensive national positioning, navigation and timing system" based on BeiDou by 2035. The system has already become operational in Pakistan following rollout of ground stations, with the military opting to switch from GPS to BeiDou services.

Licensing and Franchising

Before engaging in any form of licensing or franchising, companies are strongly advised to secure their IPR, not only in their home country but also in China. Licensing is generally defined as the permission granted by an exclusive owner of IPR such as trademarks, copyrights, technology, or patents to another party to use such IPR on agreed terms and conditions including the payment of royalties whereas the IPR owner retains ownership of the IPR. As a company grows and develops a reputation for quality services and products, its intellectual property becomes more valuable and more susceptible to counterfeiting. Nowadays, licensing and franchising are no longer reserved to multinational brand companies and niche-market businesses. Smaller businesses can also benefit from licensing and franchising agreements.

Representative Office (RO)

The RO is one of the most inexpensive and useful business vehicles through which foreign companies can establish their first China presence. It has been traditionally used as a first step to gaining a foothold in China. Its popularity is due to the relative simplicity and short time frame required to set up such an office. Compared to alternative market entry vehicles an RO is a low-risk venture as it allows a certain level of control over the company's China business activities through the employment of foreign staff and is often chosen by most Western companies as a way to advertise before expanding their commercial operations in China. Another major advantage of setting up an RO is that, for it to be operational, there is no capital requirement. This allows Western businesses on a tight budget to set up an entity in China by just paying office rental, staff salaries, and utility fees. This structure also allows foreign staff to obtain legally required residence permits and working visas as well as to legally employ foreign and local staff.

An additional benefit is that, for companies seeking to enter and sell their products in the Chinese market, an RO offers the possibility to become familiar with the Chinese market before committing to a larger investment. An RO also offers the possibility to carry out liaison activities between the headquarters and potential clients or suppliers in China. This way companies can test local demand for their products or services and devise a strategy on how to meet the specific needs of prospective consumers. Other benefits include networking and brand promotion activities while an RO also allows foreign companies to better understand the operations side of doing business in China such as costs, laws and regulations, and procurement as well as local market practices. Most importantly, it paves the way for more substantial investments by the headquarters in the future.

Supplier identifications and quality checks can also be done by the RO. That explains why the RO is a favored entry method for different types of companies and especially for Western companies procuring goods in China. In a big number of cases the RO handles sourcing and quality control activities while at the same time it is complemented by a Hong Kong or Free Trade Zone-based trading company that is in charge of the actual trading activities.

At the same time, it is important to keep in mind that the business scope of an RO is limited. ROs are legally forbidden to engage in "direct business operations." Violations may result in fines or even closure of the office. In practice, however, fines and other forms of sanctions are generally determined on a case-by-case basis. In reality, there is no clear definition of "direct business operations." On the other hand, it is very clear that the RO, being a nonlegal entity, lacks the legal standing to engage in contracts with other entities on behalf of its parent company. Certain special restrictions apply to ROs of financial institutions and other restricted types of business.

The lack of minimum capital requirement for setting up an RO ensures that the company will not engage in sales activities and focus on managing relationships with existing or potential clients. ROs are taxed in accordance with relevant regulations and they undergo an annual inspection conducted by the local tax authorities and the Administration of Industry and Commerce. Article 3 of the Administration of the Registration of Resident Representative Offices of Foreign Enterprises Procedures, from the State Administration for Industry and Commerce, provides that the RO is restricted to conduct only "nondirect business activities." However, the same article does not provide further explanation of what is included in the category of "nondirect activities."

Article 4 of the Examination, Approval and Administration of Resident Representative Offices of Foreign Implementing Rules from the MOFCOM is more specific and stipulates that a resident RO of a foreign company may engage in indirect business activities within China and conduct business activities, such as business liaison, product or service presentations, market research, and technical exchanges. While the maximum term of an RO is more than three years from the date of issue of the certificate of approval, the registration certificate is valid for one year and needs to be renewed on an annual basis. To renew its registration an RO must submit an application for renewal and an annual report of its business operations to the Chinese registration authority within 30 days prior to the expiry date. In my experience, extensions of the term of an RO are a formality.

Representative Office Business Scope

An RO may only engage in activities within its registered business scope. These are the types of activities that are permissible:

- Conducting business liaison activities with local and foreign contacts in China on behalf of the parent company
- Act as an intermediary and a coordinator for the foreign company's China activities
- Introducing the company's products or services and providing promotional materials to potential customers or trading partners
- Investigating and collecting market information, conducting market research activities for its headquarter
- Making travel arrangements for trade visits in China
- Technical exchanges
- Acting as a coordinator between the parent company and its affiliates or other associated companies

An RO may only engage in nonprofit-making activities. Under no circumstances may an RO engage in the following activities in China:

- Directly engage in business for profit
- Represent any company other than its headquarter
- Collect payments or issue invoices for services or products within China
- Import production equipment or buy property

In practice, however, many ROs provide services that are outside their framed legal scope. Local State Administration of Industry and Commerce (SAIC) branches are empowered to impose sanctions to the RO for operating without a business license or for engaging in operating activities and collecting payments through various means.

The apparent reason of limiting ROs to "nondirect business activities" is to ensure that they will act on behalf of the parent company and not on their own behalf as distinct business entities. As a result, contracts should be signed under the name of the parent enterprise or one of its affiliates in which case an address outside China is required for the relevant foreign party. Any sale, billing, or collection of money for consulting, technical, inspection, or other services should be carried out by the parent company.

You also need to make sure that you comply with the following rules:

- The RO is required to submit the annual report to the SAIC during the period of March 1 to June 30.
- The head office of the RO must have been established for at least two years before the application.
- The number of representatives is limited to four people. ROs with a larger number of representatives may only apply for de-registration but new ones cannot be added.

Investment

In addition to establishing an RO, foreign investors have several other options. These options require heavier capital investment and include:

- WOFE
- Partnerships
- JVs: Equity Joint Ventures (EJV) and Contractual Joint Ventures (CJV)

Activities that are allowed to be performed by foreign investors under the Chinese law are listed in the *2020 Catalogue of Industries for Guiding Foreign Investment.*

Preinvestment Considerations

Entering the Chinese market requires a lot of strategic planning and it is highly recommended that legal experts are consulted before the company's market entry. It is crucial to decide in advance which kind of business scope the company will have. This decision will affect the registration and the application process for obtaining the business license.

The table below shows the most common forms of investment in China.

Choices of Chinese market entry	
Form of investment	Legal standing
Representative office	No legal identity
WFOE (100% foreign investment)	LLC (limited liability company)
Joint Venture (minimum 25% foreign investment)	LLC or partnership (contractual JV)
Holding or regional headquarters	LLC
Merger and acquisition	LLC or foreign-invested company by shares
Public shares	Chinese Stock Company

Wholly Foreign-Owned Enterprise (WFOE/WOFE)

A WFOE, commonly known as "WOFE," is a limited liability company (LLC) owned by foreign nationals and capitalized solely by one or more foreign investors. The WOFE is a suitable structure for companies whose main activities in China consist in selling products, manufacturing, or providing such services as business consulting or research and development. Companies engaging in trading or retail and distribution of imported goods may also do so under a WOFE but must be registered as a specific type of WOFE known as a FICE. According to Chinese law, *"foreign investors are permitted to establish a 100 percent foreign-owned enterprise in industries that are conducive to the development of China's economic interests and not prohibited or restricted by the Chinese government."* A complete list of these categories can be found in the Investment Catalogue.

The Chinese law and regulations prohibit or restrict the creation of WFOEs in certain industries. MOFCOM, the Chinese Ministry of Commerce, is generally responsible for the examination and approval.

The typical lifespan of a WOFE is between 15 and 30 years. In case the capital is large, the construction period is long and the return on investment is low or in cases where sophisticated or internationally competitive goods using advanced technologies are produced by the foreign partner, it is possible to obtain an extension of the WOFE's duration. A WOFE can be extended up to an additional 50 years upon approval from the State Council. Advantages of choosing a WOFE as an investment vehicle include—but are not limited to—the protection of proprietary technology and other IPR, exclusive management control over all decisions and profits of the parent company without the involvement of the Chinese partner. The WOFE is the sole recipient of investment vehicle profits and is able to issue invoices to customers in RMB while it maintains full control of human resources.

Registered capital is the amount of money required by the law to establish a company. The amount varies depending on the local administration, the industry sector, the region, and the intended size of the business. This amount should be consistent with the scale of intended business operations. Increases in the amount of the registered capital must receive prior approval from the competent authorities. On the other hand, unless special approval is granted, the registered capital cannot be reduced during the term of operation. Foreign investors may contribute capital in the form of freely convertible foreign currencies or certified RMB profits from other FIEs. Items such as equipment, machinery, proprietary technology, or industrial property can also be capitalized based on their monetary value. It is important to know that the time limit within which the capital contributions are to be made must be clearly specified in the application and articles of associations. Contributions can be made in installments. The first installment must be made within 90 days of the issuance of the business license, representing no less than 15 percent of the total registered capital amount, while the last installment within 3 years. After all capital contributions have been made the company must engage a China registered accountant to verify the contributions and provide an investment verification report.

WOFEs are generally required to make allocations to a reserve fund as well as a bonus and welfare fund for their staff from the after-tax profits. Reserve fund allocations must not be less than 10 percent of the after-tax profits. Profits may not be distributed until clearance of the prior years' losses.

According to Chinese law, the minimum registered capital for a single shareholder company is RMB 100,000 while for a multiple shareholder company the minimum required capital is RMB 30,000. For a FICE the capital required is much higher. For example, the amount required for trading (import–export) rights is no less than RMB 1 million, for wholesale distribution rights the amount is generally RMB 500,000, while for retail distribution rights it is RMB 300,000. Generally, the local authorities review the feasibility study on a case-by-case basis before granting the investment approval.

Minimum registered capital	
Limited liability company (with multiple shareholders)	RMB 30,000
Limited liability company (with a single shareholder)	RMB 100,000

Total investment is the registered capital together with foreign exchange loans, usually originating from the parent company. Total investment refers to the maximum amount that the mother company is allowed to transfer to its China-based subsidiary. It is the only source the

WOFE can rely on to finance its operations until it generates profits from its business activities. It is important to know that the amount of total investment is limited and strictly supervised. For that reason it is crucial to prepare a financial plan and set the amount of total investment with a clear view on expected future costs and revenues until the WOFE can reply solely on its own profits. It is necessary to ensure that the registered capital is sufficient for the company's cash flow needs throughout the first phases of the start-up period. Moreover, careful attention should be paid to the relationship between registered capital and total investment. The financial gap, that is, the difference between registered capital and financial investment should be planned very carefully.

Joint Ventures

A JV is an LLC formed by a Chinese company and one or more foreign investors. I want to emphasize that the JV is not the result of a merger or an acquisition between a Chinese and a foreign company. The JV is a totally new entity, partly owned by both sides—with the foreign party owning at least 25 percent of the total shares. Liability does not extend to the parent company and is limited to the assets each of the parties has brought to the business. There are two types of possible JVs in China: the EJV and the CJV. Although on the surface they might appear very similar, they do have different implications for the structuring of the entity. Before committing to any JV you need to ask yourself *why* you need a partner. They should have tangible assets to contribute. Obviously, the main reason foreign companies choose to enter into a partnership with a domestic company is that the latter can be used as an entry vehicle to help them access an industrial sector which is otherwise restricted or prohibited to 100 percent foreign investment.

In fact "joint venture" sounds like a rather friendly way of doing business in China. An ideal marriage between two parties in pursuit of common goals perhaps? It is very likely that you will be offered a lot of such deals. Many Chinese companies are looking to gain access to Western technology and they are also looking to secure foreign sales through a foreign partner. This option, indeed, might sound more compelling than a WFOE, which is the main alternative. Be aware though that China's business history is full of broken dreams and unhappy partnerships. A CEO of a major Western consumer electronics company once told me that their JV was a win/win situation in the sense that the Chinese side won twice.

Remember that strategy must always lead structure. It is important to create a JV for the right reasons. In the same way it is crucial that you choose the right structure for the JV itself not because legal rules imply a particular direction but because of operational business reasons. The Chinese government still requires participation of Chinese companies in a number of sectors. This might be one reason why your company would prefer this structure while an alternative one is that Chinese partners are used because they have valuable assets to offer, such as a well-established distribution network, brand reputation, technical know-how for a special manufacturing process, or other forms of tangible assets such as special licenses or even land use rights.

It is a common mistake to think that a JV will limit your cost of market entry due to the shared costs. Experience shows it is usually far from being the case. Another important question you should think is what the partner wants or expects out of this partnership. It is equally important to engage in thorough discussions with them in order to understand their perspective which might be very different from what you might be thinking.

Below you can see a checklist of the main issues you will need to consider:

- What will your company's business scope be?
- FIEs as well as local companies have to operate within their business scope. In China, this question is more critical than in most Western countries.
- Does your business fall within the "encouraged," "permitted," "restricted," or "prohibited" industry category? This will determine whether you are allowed to set up a WFOE or a JV and will lead you to study and consider the available options and incentives.
- What should the registered capital and total investment amounts be? This is a crucial issue that needs to be planned

based on an organizational not a legal perspective. At this stage don't feel limited by any regulatory restrictions.

- How would you arrange profit distributions and the sharing of responsibility in case of losses?
- What taxes will you need to pay? Some of these taxes will be business tax, VAT, foreign enterprise income tax, individual income tax, withholding tax, and customs duties.
- Which location should you choose to establish your company? Depending on your sectoral needs you will have several location options around the country, possibly including development zones with various characteristics and incentives.
- The texts of the articles of association. These will determine issues like profits repatriation, board structure, trade unions, as well as liquidation.
- Some additional points to consider relating to the specifics of JVs include:
  o Who will be the leading party in the daily running of the business?
  o Who will be in charge of local sales or export sales?
  o Is it fine to allow one party to increase the registered capital unilaterally?

Equity Joint Ventures

An EJV is a legal entity created by Chinese and foreign partners that hold joint ownership and operations of an LLC and have reached an agreement on management and the division of profit and risk. EJV companies share both revenues and risks based on their respective registered capital contributions. The foreign party's capital in an EJV must account for at least 25 percent of the total registered capital. According to the Investment Catalogue, in specific industries, the Chinese party is required to have control over the JV in which case the foreign side is not permitted to own more than 49 percent. Profit is distributed based on each party's respective ownership interest, normally in the form of dividends.

The steps to follow for approval of an EJV are generally very similar to the WFOE. The list of required documents differs though, since in this case a JV contract is required. The necessary steps also depend on the industry in which your business operates and the required special permits. However, the time needed to set up an EJV is usually longer compared to the setup of a WFOE. Approval from MOFCOM is generally granted at the central level but a proposed EJV can apply to the provincial bureau in case certain requirements are met, such as the ones listed below:

- The business scope is aligned with the encouraged categories listed in the Investment Catalogue.
- Total investment is less than RMB 1 million.
- The EJV is self-financed.
- It does not affect foreign trade quotas.
- It does not require China to allocate additional raw materials.

Capital contributions of an EJV can take the form of cash, industrial property rights, capital goods, and other assets. Generally, the Chinese partner will contribute cash land or land use rights, while the foreign partner will most likely contribute cash, equipment, machinery, or construction materials. All JV contracts must contain a schedule for capital contributions. In case the capital contribution is made in a single payment all partners must complete the payment of the full amount within six months of the date the business license is issued. A temporary business license is normally issued during the capital contributions period. If the partners fail to make their contributions within the required time frame, the temporary license will not be renewed. All capital contributions must be certified in an official report from a China-registered Certified Public Accountant (CPA) firm as a way to confirm that the contributions stated in the contract have been received. During the life of an EJV the foreign partner's equity contribution should generally not be repaid. Once the venture has been liquidated though, the net assets—if there are any—will be distributed according to the shareholdings of each partner.

Regarding the relationship between the shareholders, the partners of an EJV share joint management of the whole venture and representation matches the proportion of shareholder interest in the venture. The board of directors holds the power to make all major decisions regarding the financial standing of the venture. Partners share common responsibility in the appointment of the board members and a board meeting is required at least once a year according to the law. Also, the board of directors must engage a general manager and deputy managers. The general manager will be responsible for board decisions as well as for the daily management of the venture.

The profits and losses of an EJV are distributed based on the ratio of each partner's investment. After taxes have been paid and profits distributed, the JV is required to make allocations to three funds: a welfare and staff bonus fund, a general reserve fund, and an enterprise expansion fund. Normally, the amount to these three funds is designated in the JV contract or it must be decided by the board of directors. Note that all losses from previous years must be cleared before distributing the current year's profits.

Cooperative/Contractual Joint Ventures

A cooperative joint venture or CJV is a partnership between a Chinese organization or enterprise and a foreign organization, enterprise, or individual. A CJV can take the form of a partnership based on an incorporated arrangement with an LLC while it can also be based on a contractual cooperation agreement (real CJV). It is important to mention that there are not many real CJVs. What is of benefit to the foreign party is that they can enjoy a lot of flexibility when negotiating the specifics of the CJV and enjoy an important bargaining power for profit sharing, capital investment, management structure, and so on. There is a minimum of 25 percent of foreign investment required in the CJV while there is no limit for the contribution of the Chinese party. Ownership as well as profit or losses of a CJV are usually not shared on an equity or capital contributions basis but are determined on the basis of a contractual agreement between the parties involved.

The CJV contract should state each investor's obligations in terms of invested capital as well as timeline. If an investor fails to fulfill their contract obligations SAIC will set a new timeline for carrying out those engagements. An investor who fails to fulfill their capital obligations might be charged with breach of contract. EJVs are required to have a registered capital which will be the total amount of capital registered with SAIC at the time of the establishment of the EJV. The amount should be stated clearly in RMB unless of course both parties agree on an alternative currency.

Capital contributed to the venture by all involved parties may be in cash or kind. Industrial property rights, land use rights, as well as other property rights can be used as capital contributions. The law on CJVs requires that all parties fulfill their investment and cooperation obligations as these are stated in the JV contract. Failure to do so within the prescribed time frame will lead to another deadline being set by the relevant authorities whereas further failure will be handled based on the relevant state provisions. Capital contributions must be verified by a Chinese-registered CPA which will issue a verification certificate. As in the case of the EJV, a CJV, as an LLC, must appoint a board of directors or a joint managerial committee that will be in charge of making all major decisions and supervise the management of the JV.

The profits and losses of a CJV would normally be distributed following the ratio stated in the contract. This varies over the contract terms. Note that the total amount provided by an EJV for the three reserve funds (general reserve fund, staff bonus and welfare fund, and enterprise expansion fund) is expressed as a percentage of the after-tax profits, while in the case of the CJV the total amount provided to these funds is expressed as a percentage of pretax profits.

WFOE		JV	
Pro's	Con's	Pro's	Con's
Fast decision making processes	Capital contribution only from one party	Capital from 2 or more parties	Time and cost expenditure because of more effort and longer decision-making process
Protected technologies and know-how	Limited knowledge of the Chinese market	Share of the costs and the risk	Technology and know-how piracy risk
100% ownership and control	Built-up relationships with Chinese business contacts and government long-term process	Use relationships of Chinese JV partner and his business and government contacts	Dependency
No culture differences			Culture differences

Foreign-Invested Commercial Enterprise

Once an international company has reached a level of success in trading with or selling to China, it is only natural that they decide to establish an on-the-ground presence, usually in the form of a FICE. This structure has become one of the most popular ones among foreign investors who wish to enter the Chinese market as it is by far the most convenient and cost-efficient business structure available to foreign traders seeking to:

- Import goods to China for direct sale (either retail or wholesale)
- Establish a fully operational China-based sales and after-sales platform
- Expand their sourcing platform and be directly in charge of logistics and quality control
- Act as a liaison office for their overseas headquarters, including setting up other branches and employing staff on a national basis
- Act as an intermediary between Chinese suppliers and foreign China-based customers through the reselling of finished or semi-finished products

In fact, a FICE is easier to set up compared to a full manufacturing WFOE because the capitalization requirements are normally lower due to the absence of any imported tooling requirements or machinery. FICEs are also a more cost-effective option in comparison with ROs. From an accounting, tax, and legal perspective though, establishing a FICE demands both administrative and technical knowledge. It is crucial to ensure right from the start that the business model is feasible and that all investors have a full and very clear understanding of the internal control processes, company cash flows, as well as pre- and postregistration procedures.

A FICE is capable of conducting the commercial activities listed below. The business scope of a FICE includes one or more of the following activities:

- Import and export of goods
- Franchising

- Retailing
- Wholesaling
- Commission agency activities

There are two main types of FICE: wholesale FICE and retail FICE. A retail FICE can engage in:

- Retail of goods
- Import of goods
- Purchase of domestic products for export
- Ancillary business activities

A wholesale FICE can engage in:

- Wholesale of goods
- Import and export of goods
- Commission agency activities
- Ancillary business activities

Finally, a FICE can authorize others to open branches through way of franchising.

Foreign-Invested Partnership (FIP)

An FIP is an unlimited liability business entity without minimum registered capital requirements. It was back in 2010 when the Administrative Measures on the Establishment of Partnership Enterprises by Foreign Enterprises or Individuals in China were made official by China's State Council. For the first time, these measures opened the door for foreign investors and entities to invest directly in China-based partnerships.

The partners or investors of an FIP can be composed of:

- Two more foreign individuals or enterprises
- Foreign individuals or enterprises and Chinese natural and legal persons or other organizations

Two forms are recognized: general partnerships and limited partnerships. The measures governing the formation and arrangements of such partnerships are pretty similar to those in other countries. FIPs have become particularly popular in recent years as the most convenient and easy way for foreign investors to establish a business in China. In addition to be an attractive entry strategy for private equity funds, FIPs are open to all "encouraged" sectors of the Investment Catalogue and also to certain restrictive sectors subject to review.

Registration of an FIP is subject to the following requirements:

- It is not forbidden to invest in all prohibited industries listed in the Investment Catalogue.
- In case an FIP intends to invest in areas stated as "restricted" in the Investment, it will be subject to a close examination by the SAIC which will seek the opinion of relevant departments before granting any approval.
- FIPs are not permitted to invest in industries "restricted to JVs" or where it is required that a Chinese party holds a controlling interest.
- The establishment of an FIP must first be approved and registered with the industry and commerce bureaus of the province, municipality, or autonomous region directly under the central government or subdivision where the investors intend to establish the business.
- Unlike ROs, FIPs do not need annual re-registration. An FIP can have a term of 15 to 30 years.

When setting up an FIP there is no minimum requirement of registered capital. However, it is necessary to submit a confirmation of agreed consideration signed by all partners or an assessment certificate of consideration issued by a China-registered statutory agency. Current measures allow FIP partners to contribute capital in local or foreign currency. All FIP parties may also contribute to the FIP's capital in terms of intellectual property or land use rights or even labor investments. Note that only the general partner is allowed to make capital contributions by labor service, always following certain regulations. A foreign general partner making contributions by labor investment must submit employment licenses of all foreign staff to the competent SAIC branch.

Profits of an FIP can be distributed in the following ways:

- As agreed in the partnership agreement
- According to the decision of the partners
- Based on the share of capital contribution made by each partner
- Equally among all partners

An FIP is generally seen as a flow-through entity and for that reason income tax is imposed at the partner level. A legal person/partner is subject to a 3 percent to 5 percent business and corporate income tax (CIT) for the profits they receive.

Joint Stock Companies

The foreign-invested joint stock company, also known as a company limited by shares, is a particularly attractive option because it allows for broad participation in the equity of the company, whether it is a foreign or domestic company and whether it is private or public. This structure type offers its executives and employees stock incentive plans and eventually also offers its shares on a public stock exchange (e.g., Beijing or Shanghai Stock Exchange). Moreover, it can use its stock as assets or currency in debt and equity offerings as well as mergers and acquisitions. From that perspective the FIJSC is very similar to its corporate counterparts in the United States and Europe.

Greater freedom to enlist broader participation in its equity comes along with higher and more demanding requirements of corporate governance. Therefore, the minimum capital requirement is also substantially higher (RMB 30 million). Given that the FIJSC is a more complex organization, it requires more time, energy, and financial resources to establish. On the other hand, for foreign-invested companies seeking to conduct the full range of corporate activities which are normally associated with growing and ambitious Western companies, the FIJSC offers the most suitable structure.

Other recently introduced foreign company structures also offer the opportunity to comingle assets with Chinese partners but these companies are purposely designed for investing, and not for business operations, and reach beyond the means of most businesses. These include the foreign-invested holding company and foreign-invested venture capital investment enterprise. The minimum cumulative capital requirement is U.S.$30 million for the former and the standard requirement for the latter is that each investor contributes a minimum of U.S.$1 million.

Due to certain limitations to the traditional business structures, including the inability to coinvest with Chinese partners, the most flexible and versatile FIP and FIJSC offer investors some tantalizing options. The complexity of the FIJSC and the novelty and lack of familiarity of the partnership can potentially lead some to turn back to the WFOE structure. However, it is likely a matter of time until the FIPs and FIJSCs become a more popular choice among foreign and domestic investors in China.

Foreign Investment Structures in China

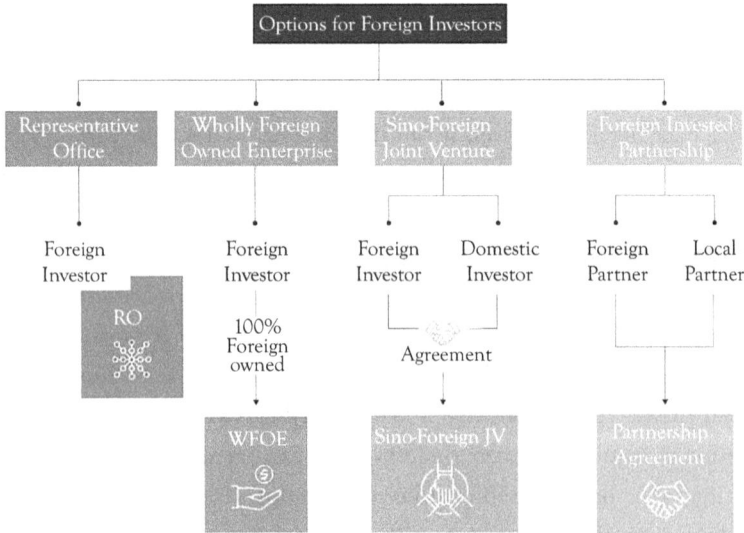

Comparative Analysis of Different Investment Vehicle Structures

Investment vehicle	Common purpose	Separate legal status	Taxation	Setup procedure	Pros	Cons
Representative Office (RO)	• Market research • liaise with overseas headquarters	x	On expenditure	• Pre-Licensing = 1-2 months • Post-Licensing = 1-2 months	• Easiest foreign Investment structure to set up • No registered capital requirement • Paves way for future investment	• Cannot invoice locally in RMB • Must recruit staff from local agency, no more than four foreign representatives • Heavily taxed if expenses are high • Parent company must be 2 years old or more
Wholly Foreign-Owned Enterprise (WFOE)	• Manufacturing • Servicing • Trading	✓	On revenue	• Pre-Licensing = 2-3 months • Post-Licensing = 2-3 months	• 100% ownership and management control • Greater freedom in business activities than RO	• Registered capital requirement for selected industries • Longer establishment process than RO • Barred from access to some industries
Sino-Foreign Joint Venture (JV)	• Entering into restricted industries (which by law require a local partner) • Leveraging a local partner's existing hard assets and soft resources	✓	On revenue	• Pre-Licensing = 2-3 months • Post-Licensing = 2-3 months	• Allows foreign investors entry into restricted industries • Local and foreign partners can share assets, resources, knowledge; risk and costs between them	• Profit sharing • Loss of full control • Technology transfer/IP risks • Inheriting partner libilities
Foreign-Ivested Partnerships (FIP)	• Investment vehicle • Servicing	x	Partners pay tax on their profits (CIT for companies; IT for individuals)	• Pre-Licensing = 2-3 months • Post-Licensing = 2-3 months	• Allows for domestic and foreign ownership • Easier setup	• Unlimited libility for the general partner • Potential challenges with taxation or foreign currency exchanges due to newness of structure

Mergers and Acquisitions

Purchasing a company can be a difficult process in China. However, for some foreign companies this can be the right path to accelerate growth. In fact, in certain situations, acquiring a Chinese company can be much more effective than starting from scratch and relying solely on organic growth. Many advantages and drawbacks of setting up a JV with a Chinese partner also apply to a company acquisition. Some of the advantages include access to already established customer relationships and local professional networks, as well as local business knowledge and distribution channels.

The Chinese government generally maintains an influential role in any domestic company acquisition. If a foreign investor wants to purchase a Chinese company, an approval is needed by a number of government bodies. In 2011 a new regulation came into effect aimed at controlling foreign purchases of domestic companies. In fact, acquisitions of majority shares in certain highly regulated industries which are of strategic importance to the Chinese government, such as defense, energy, infrastructure, food and technology, have to pass a special review by the Council of State, the National Development and Reform Commission, the Ministry of Commerce, and other government agencies. Approval normally takes a significant amount of time and effort and depends on a large variety of factors (e.g., industry, investment values, current status of the acquired company).

Relevant government bodies include:

The *Ministry of Commerce (MOFCOM)*, responsible for supervising and approving company acquisitions.

The *State Owned Assets Supervision and Administration Commission (SASAC)*, responsible for supervising and managing state-owned assets of companies under government supervision.

The *State Development and Reform Commission (SDRC)*, responsible for approving any foreign project applications.

The *China Securities Regulatory Commission (CSRC)*, responsible for regulating China's securities and future markets. Companies listed on China's stock market need to receive approval from the CSRC.

Depending always on the industry sector (this especially applies to highly regulated industries) approval from industry-specific bodies might also be required. When elaborating an acquisition strategy, it is recommended to spend a good amount of time looking for suitable acquisition candidates and to develop a clear and well-defined plan for successfully integrating the company after acquisition. When developing such strategies, foreign investors should consider:

- Whether the available capital is sufficient
- Whether other company resources (e.g., human resources) are sufficient or adequate
- New laws and regulations and their possible implications for the company
- Market size and competitors
- Cultural differences
- Compatibility with the domestic company

Absence of a well-thought thorough merger strategy is likely to result in future trouble with the target company or even lead to total failure and costs.

There are two main ways of acquiring a Chinese company or parts of it: equity acquisition and asset acquisition. Choosing the right acquisition form depends on several factors, including legal and tax consequences as well as the financial standing of the domestic company. Equity acquisition is the most common way of acquiring a company in China. The foreign investor acquires equity of a Chinese or, in certain cases, an existing foreign-invested company. As mentioned above, that requires approval from various local authorities. In case the acquisition target is a FIE, approval needs to be granted by the authorities that were involved in the formation of that company. If the target is a Chinese company, it will need to be converted into a FIE and the conversion needs to be approved by the relevant government bodies. The reason this is a popular form of acquisition is that purchasing equity is usually the most convenient and fastest way of acquiring a company in China. It is essential to bear in mind that in an equity acquisition situation the buying company also "acquires" the obligations and liabilities of the target company. Should that company have a lot of debts or other financial obligations, the buyer could potentially be exposed to high risks.

An alternative method is to acquire selected assets of the target company. This option enables the foreign investor to cherry-pick the target company's best or most valuable assets. There is no charge of equity ownership. The acquiring company normally buys some parts of the target company without the need for governmental approval regarding the transfer of the assets. Know, however, that in order to purchase any assets in China, a foreign company has to be legally established, which, again, is a process requiring approval by many government agencies. Generally, asset acquisition is a more time-consuming process than equity acquisition. The advantage, however, is that liabilities of the target company are not assumed by the buyer, hence considerably reducing the risks associated with an acquisition. As opposed to an equity acquisition, all business and employment contracts related to the acquired assets need to be renegotiated and signed by the buying company, which can be a cumbersome process. Moreover, the seller will have to pay higher taxes which, in turn, might be passed on to the buyer. Additionally, if the target company is a FIE and sells its assets, money saved from preferential tax treatments can be claimed back from the government in case the conditions for receiving the incentive have changed.

Establishing and Running a Business in China

Preparation

Different local authorities will be involved at different stages of the approval procedure for all foreign entities. Throughout the incorporation process you will become familiar with departments such as the AIC (Administration of Industry and Commerce), the BOFTEC (Bureau of Foreign Trade and Economic Cooperation) also known under the name of "Foreign Investment Bureau" in some provincial cities, the administrative committees of development zones, the state and local tax bureaus, and customs. The establishment procedure typically goes through central, provincial, and local-level authority approvals depending on the sector the company is involved and the amount of the intended total investment as well as the establishment location. MOFCOM, the Ministry of Commerce, is the final approval authority for a WFOE or a JV but it delegates part of its power to local counterparts such as the BOFTEC at municipality and provincial levels. Specific industry categories might require additional licensing which usually needs to be obtained at the outset.

Establishing a foreign investment structure in China normally takes between three and six months. The establishment process can vary depending on the foreign investment structures and the intended business scope. As a reference, manufacturing WFOEs usually require an environmental evaluation report; WFOEs involved in trading will have to go through customs/commodity inspection registration. Registered capital requirements vary among different structures. A few years ago, establishing service or consulting WFOEs officially required a minimum of RMB 100,000 and FICEs a minimum of RMB 500,000 due to value-added tax (VAT) purposes. Since 2016 no defined minimum capital is required. In practice, however, capital is still needed but the good news is that it is more flexible for a company to set its own level. Remember that despite these regulation changes, it remains important to set capital levels correctly from the outset as it could be very costly not to do so.

There are many issues to consider before making any firm decision to establish an entity in China. It can be hard to be aware of all the implications, especially if you are trying to make this decision based only on a few visits. Make sure you spend a fair amount of time in China before committing to any form of investment.

Type	Chinese partner	Advantages	IPR	Human resources	Investment risk	Government issues	Purpose
Rep office	No Chinese partner	Traditionally easy to establish	Marketing and R&D activities only, IPR kept by headquarter	Limited to four expatriates	Low	Increasingly strict enforcement to ensure compliance with regulations	Liaison with home office / relationship building and market research
Partnerships	One or more	Easy to establish No corporate tax	Optional	To be decided by parties	Low, no capital requirements, However, unlimited liability and subject to individual income tax	New regulations are encouraging	Option for smaller businesses looking for an easy set-up, willing to have a partner and take on unlimited liability
Wholly foreign -owned enterprise	No Chinese partner	Efficient in operations, management and future development; easier to terminate than JVs	More control over IPR and technology	Full control of human resources	High investment risk, no Chinese partner, FICEs (foreign-invested commercial enterprise) have higher capital requirements	In some cases, government incentives more difficult to obtain without Chinese partner	Manufacturing Services FICE: Commerce, retail, distribution
Equity joint venture	One or more	Foreign partners can gain market knowledge, contacts, preferential market treatment and manufacturing capability from their Chinese partner	Chinese partner will gain full access to the foreign IPR	Advised to retain key positions in board of directors and management (risk management, finance, HR) Use of local talent	Risk based on the equity shares of each partner (foreign and Chinese)	The foreign partner must contribute a minimum of 25% of registered capital (there are exceptions for some restricted industries)	Only option in some sectors according to the Investment Catalogue Establishment of a close partnership
Contractual joint venture	One or more	Depend on terms set in the contract	Based on the contract	Based on the contract	Contributions can be made in form of labour or property	No minimum contribution to be made by the foreign partner	Only option in some sectors according to the Investment Catalogue Establishment of a close partnership

Necessary Documents

You need to get familiar with some documents that will be required during the establishment process. Below I am listing and then giving a general description of the most commonly required documents:

- Articles of association
- Shareholders agreement in case of more than one investor
- Environmental Protection Evaluation Report

- Ownership certificate or lease contract for premises along with a certificate of land use rights if necessary
- Appointment letter for the legal representative and photocopy of their passport
- Appointment letter for the general manager, CV and photocopy of their passport

Feasibility Study

A feasibility study is a detailed analysis of the company's business plan that will be submitted and carefully studied by the Chinese authorities in charge of the approval. The competent authorities will check whether the claimed aims are realistic, in favor of the Chinese market and the growth of the Chinese economy and whether the financial, human, and other allocated resources are sufficient. It is an important document and it should be given a lot of attention. The feasibility study should describe the purpose of the business, the intended activities, its products or services, the technology and equipment that will be used, the land area needed, and all the related requirements, conditions, and quantities of natural resources, electricity, water and other energy resources needed as well as all the requirements of public facilities use.

Articles of Association

This is a document that describes the cornerstones of the enterprise and its operation. The importance of this document should not be underestimated because its content can facilitate your operation or make it more difficult. The articles of association will not only be needed for the initial approval but also for every important change during the whole life of the company, such as changes in the number of board directors, an increase of the registered capital, possible liquidation of the company or profit repatriation. The minimum content must include the following:

- Name and registered address of the company
- Purpose and scope of the enterprise

- Total amount of investment, registered capital, and time frame for capital subscription
- Form of the company
- Establishment of the internal departments and their functions, powers and procedure rules, duties and power limits of the legal representative and relevant employees.
- Labor management
- Principles and system of financial affairs, accounting, and auditing
- Operating period, termination, and liquidation of the enterprise
- Procedures for amending the articles of association

Environmental Protection Evaluation Report

This report is required especially for manufacturing companies and FICEs and must contain information on raw materials, equipment and machinery, safe disposal of toxic products, and all information regarding the company's activities likely to have an impact on the environment. Note that the complete list of documents and application forms, language, and notarization requirements can be found out by direct request at the local administrative office in addition to the above documents. I strongly recommend to hire a legal advisor as the requirements differ among industries, authorities, and locations.

How to Establish a Representative Office

Having a physical presence in China can be part of a long-term strategy to enter the Chinese market and it can generally be done within just a couple of months. To register and set up an RO a company must register with the Chinese Administration of Industry and Commerce, a process which usually takes about three months. In general, the application and registration process takes two weeks and the whole RO set-up normally takes about two months. Although the process can be easier if you already have an existing company established in your home country, newly incorporated companies can also be used to register an RO, in which case you must provide a bank reference for application purposes at the local bureaus.

All foreign companies applying to establish an RO must comply with the following stipulated criteria:

- Be legally registered in their home country.
- Enjoy a "good business reputation."
- Provide reliable and authentic documents as required by the relevant laws and regulations.
- Be in charge of the relevant establishment procedures according to the relevant laws and regulations.

Moreover, depending on which industry and business category your company falls into, the relevant government approval bodies may insist that the applicant has been in business for a specified period of time which is usually one year and may also ask them to provide evidence of past business dealings between the applicant and China. Generally these requirements are flexible and can be met by the company after careful preparation.

Key Features

An RO has no legal standing, meaning that it does not possess the capacity for civil rights and conduct, cannot assume civil liability independently of the parent company, and is fairly limited in its hiring ability. No more than four foreign employees can be hired while local staff can only be hired through government HR agencies.

To establish an RO the steps below need to be followed:

You will need to:

1. Acquire preliminary approval from the relevant government authority. Since the circular issued in 2004 by the State Council, foreign companies engaging in consulting, trade, investing, manufacturing, advertising, and goods transportation and leasing do not need to be approved by MOFCOM. After the elimination of the preliminary approval requirement, the procedure has been significantly simplified. However, approval from other authorities is still required for ROs of foreign companies operating within specific industries. For instance, foreign financial institutions and banking enterprises are overseen by the China Banking Regulatory Commission.
2. Register with the Administration of Industry and Commerce to receive the Registration Certificate for Representative Office of Foreign Enterprises (Hong Kong, Macao, and Taiwan).
3. Apply for official and carving chops (Financial and RO chop) and register with the Public Security Bureau.
4. Apply at the Bureau of Quality and Technology Supervision for the Enterprise Code.
5. Apply for local tax registration.
6. Apply for state tax registration.
7. Apply for approval at the People's Bank of China to open a foreign exchange bank account.
8. Open bank accounts (foreign exchange current account and basic RMB account).
9. Enter into employment contract with the designated departments under the labor bureau or with Foreign Enterprise Service Company Organization (FESCO) or other licensed HR agencies.

There is no need to have an accredited local agent—Shanghai being an exception—to be in charge of the application process. Anybody can submit the application to the Administration of Industry and Commerce. However, considering the special documents required it is likely that the application will be returned several times making the whole process particularly time consuming. Although it is not a request to do the registration application using a foreign-service unit, I recommend businesses to use an accredited Chinese agent if they want to get a successful RO registration and save time. For the sake of giving you an average service cost, in Beijing the average cost charged for RO registration is RMB 11,200 while in Shanghai it is about RMB 10,000.

Establishing a representative office

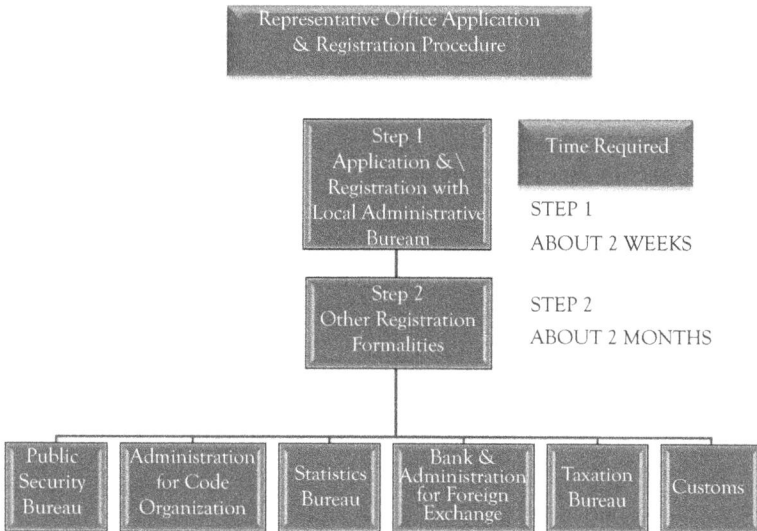

Required Documents

The main documents required to be submitted with the application for the establishment of a foreign party's RO are listed below. However, approval authorities may require additional documents.

1. An application letter signed and sealed by the general manager or the chairman of the board of directors.

2. Notarized copies of the constitutional and supportive documents sanctioning the legal incorporation and operation of the company provided by the authorities of the jurisdiction where the foreign company was established. These include: Incorporation or Business Registration Certificate of holding company, Annual Report, and Tax Statements.

3. Bank reference letter providing basic information about the applicant (name, legal address, date of opening of the corporate account, registered capital, credit standing, and overall comments made by the bank).

4. Official premises lease or purchase contract together with the landlord, property certificate, and letter of appointment addressed to the chief representative.

5. Identity certificate (ID, passport copy, and visa) of the chief representative.

6. Resume of the chief representative with their signature.

7. Photo of the chief representative.

Post-Setup Registration and Filing Procedure

After a foreign company's RO application is approved and they have received the company's Registration Certificate, Chinese law requires the RO, and in some cases its personnel, to carry out a number of administrative registrations and filings. It usually takes 20 working days for the Approval Certificate to be issued, starting from the time of receiving full particulars, instructions, and documents from the applicant. The post-setup registration procedure should take around 40 working days.

The standard post-setup procedures prescribed by the national authorities are set out here.

Public Security Bureau (PSB)

A. Within 10 days of the issuance of the Registration Certificate, the RO is required to file with the local public security bureau. The documents needed for the PSB to issue a Filling and Registration Record are:
   - The approval letter
   - The Registration Certificate

Office Chops

The RO is further required to apply for office chops with the competent local PSB and has to provide the following documents:

- Application letter signed by the company's legal representative
- Filling and Registration Record
- One original and one photocopy of personal identification or passport ID of the individual authorized to apply to make the chop.

The PSB will allow the RO to have the chops made at a designated unit.

TSB—Technical Supervision Vision

The RO has to apply for the enterprise organization code with the local TSB and has to provide the following documents:

- Application form
- Registration Certificate, one original and one copy
- One copy of ID of the chief representative of the RO
- Approval Certificate
- Office chop

The local TSB will issue a Certificate of Enterprise Organization Code, also known as IC card, providing one original, one copy, and one electronic copy.

State Administration of Foreign Exchange (SAFE)

The RO has to register with the local Administration of Foreign Exchange. The following documents have to be submitted:

- Registration form
- Registration Certificate
- Approval letter
- Approval Certificate

- Certificate of Enterprise Organization Code
- Office chop

The AFE will issue a Foreign Exchange Account License and a Foreign Exchange Registration Certificate.

Local Bank

The RO must open an RMB and a foreign exchange local bank account. The following items are required:

- Registration Certificate
- Approval letter
- Approval Certificate
- Certificate of Enterprise Organization Code
- Foreign Exchange Account License
- Foreign Exchange Registration Certificate
- Evidence of Tax Registration
- The RO chop, finance chop, and the chief representative's chop
- ID (one original + one copy) of the legal representative
- Introduction letter of RO
- ID (one original + one copy) of each individual of the company's finance employees authorized to open corporate accounts

After submission of these documents the bank will issue account books for an RMB account and a foreign exchange account.

Tax Bureau

The RO has to register within 30 days of the issuance of the Registration Certificate with the local tax bureau. The documents that need to be submitted are given below. After submission of these documents the tax bureau will issue a State Tax Registration Certificate and a Local Tax Registration Certificate.

- Registration Certificate
- Approval letter
- Evidence of Bank Account (normally the RO account book)
- Certificate of Enterprise Organization Code
- ID of the individual filing the application

Procedures with Regard to Foreign Staff

ROs planning to employ foreign nationals are required to comply with the following procedures:

A. Directly obtain the Work Permit from the Local Labor and Social Security Bureau on submission of these documents:
    - CV of the prospective foreign employee
    - Employment Proposal
    - Report on the reason of employing a foreign person for the job
    - The prospective employee's qualification for the job
    - Health status of the prospective employee
    - Employer's business Approval Certificate
    - Five passport photos
    - Any additional documents required by Chinese laws and regulations
B. Apply for a Working Visa from the Chinese embassy in the foreign employee's home country.
C. After arrival of the foreign employee in China, he or she must apply to obtain the Working Certificate from the local LSSB on submission of the following documents:
    - Employment Contract
    - Work Permit
    - Passport
    - Five passport photos
    - Within 30 days after arrival of the employee in China they shall apply to the local PSB for a Foreign Residence Permit on submission of the Working Certificate.

Overview—RO setup procedure

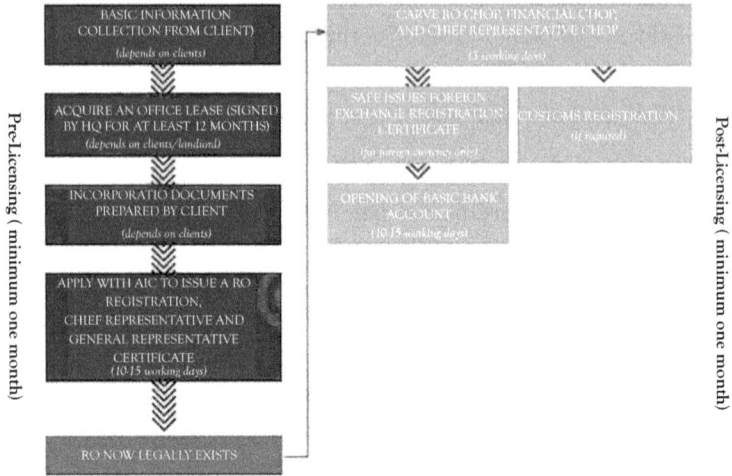

How to Establish a Wholly Foreign-Owned Enterprise (WFOE)

A business license is always required to complete the registration of a WOFE. The date of establishment of the enterprise is the date of the issuance of the business license. It's only after the application for such a license has been approved that the registration is successfully completed. The whole process usually takes at least 4 months but, depending on the company's business scope, investment amount, timely and accurate submission of the required documents it may take up to a year.

Before applying to establish a WFOE, the investor(s) must submit a report including specific information requested to the local authorities of the location where the company is set to be established. The investor will usually receive a written response within 30 days from the submission. The investor must apply for registration in order to obtain a business license within 30 days of receiving the Approval Certificate. Otherwise, the Approval Certificate will become void after this period.

Key Features

Prior to submitting the application to set up a WFOE, the foreign investor must rent an office space for the WFOE. The reason is that the lease contract is one of the documents necessary for the company registration. The contract can be concluded using the name of the parent company which can later be changed to the WFOE's name. The WFOE office cannot be placed in a residential building.

The official name must be registered with SAIC (the local Administrative Bureau for Industry and Commerce) and must be in Chinese. The proposed name must contain the following four components: (a) location, (b) enterprise name, (c) industry, and (d) company structure (e.g., LLC, LTD). In case 50 percent of the registered capital comes from foreign investors the name can be formed as "company name"+ "industry"+ "location" + "company structure" such as in this example: ABC Consulting (Shanghai) LTD.

The company needs to receive approval by the Administrative Bureau for Industry and Commerce on the proposed name of the WFOE before its formal registration. Below I am listing the restrictions on the use of company names:

- It should be in Chinese.
- Foreign alphabets and characters and Arabic numerals are not allowed.
- Content should not conflict with national policies, social ethics, and local culture.
- Content should not damage fair competition or mislead the public.
- Unless competent authorities grant approval, the following words should not be contained in the name: "China," "Chinese," "National," "State." "International" is a restricted word unless it is used to represent the industry in which the business is operating. For example, "ABC International Trading Limited."

Application

Prior to submitting the application to set up a WFOE, foreign investors must rent an office space for the company because a lease contract is one of the main documents required for registration. The lease contract can be signed by the parent company and later changed to the WFOE's name. The registered address will be the official and legal address of the company and will determine in which administrative and tax district the company will be attached. On the other hand, a WFOE is not required to operate at the registered office. It is possible to operate at a different business address.

Applying for a WFOE involves three steps:

Step 1: Application with the local Administrative Bureau for Industry and Commerce for the intended name to be used by the WFOE.

Step 2: Application for the approval of the proposed investment with the Foreign Economic Relations and Trade Bureau upon submission of the approval of feasibility study and constitution documents (articles of association and memorandum).

You need to prepare a feasibility study covering financing, technological progress, site selection, equipment, market surveys, raw material supplies, targeted figures, foreign exchange, infrastructure facilities, and so on. The company should also prepare and submit the articles of association to the examination and approval authority which usually replies within 30 days following submission. After approval of the feasibility report and of the articles of association the company shall apply to the authority in charge of issuing the Approval Certificate, within three days after receiving the application.

Step 3: Registration with the Administration Bureau of Industry and Commerce within 30 days after receiving the Approval Certificate and application for the business license. The license should normally be issued within 10 working days. It is highly recommended to use a local agent authorized by the Shanghai Municipal Foreign Economic Relations and Trade Committee to be in charge of the application procedure.

Required Documents

Local authorities work on an "approval system" instead of a "registration system" basis, which means that the application might be rejected without any specific reason. It is important that all the documentation required by the government authorities is fully and accurately submitted. Make sure that a certified translation by an approved translator or a translation agency is included for the documents that are not written in Chinese. Also, notarization of statutory documents of the mother company might also be required.

The applicant must complete the "Form for Establishing a Wholly Owned Foreign Enterprise" and submit it along with the following documents:

1. A formal application letter duly signed by the chairman of the board of directors or by the general manager of the foreign

company, including these details: name of the WFOE, name of the company's legal representative, business scope, duration, and address

2. Statutory documents of the parent company issued by the authorities of the country or region of origin such as Certificate of Incorporation, Constitution, Business Certificate, and Tax Certificate.

3. A letter issued by a bank certifying the company's credit and financial standing

4. A full list of the Legal Representatives and their CVs

5. A feasibility report

It normally takes 60 days for the local authorities to issue the Approval Certificate. The postestablishment registration procedure also takes about 60 days.

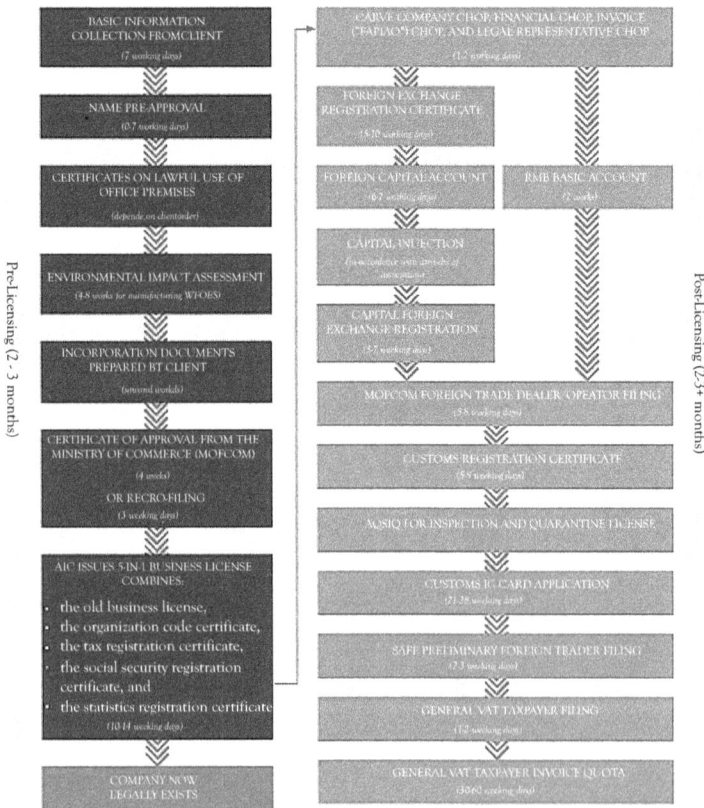

How to Establish a Joint Venture (JV)

Key Features

As with the above foreign entities, different authorities will be involved at different stages of the approval procedure of a JV in China. To set up a CJV the Chinese and foreign partners must submit documents such as a project proposal, the contract, the signed agreement, and articles of association to the relevant local government authority for examination and approval. After receiving approval, the partners have 30 days to apply for registration and a business license to the Administration of Industry and Commerce. The date of the establishment of the JV is the date on which the business license is issued. Once the establishment stage has been completed and the license obtained, the venture must register with the tax authorities within a maximum period of 30 days.

The Application Process

The application process for establishing a JV involves two main stages: the preregistration stage and the postregistration stage. Both stages are done at provincial or municipal levels although input from local offices or other state-level authorities might also be required.

Preregistration

Name Preapproval

As in the case of the WFOE setup, the SAIC is the relevant approval authority for JVs. Verification of feasibility of the proposed company name by SAIC usually takes a couple of working days. Only the Chinese name is legally binding as the English name is not legally relevant. Certain words, like the word "China," cannot be included in the Chinese name of the company. The company name can be translated based on the meaning or phonetically. For a complete list of words that cannot be used, check in the WFOE section. It is important to spend enough time to obtain an appropriate translation of the company name in Chinese and use it as a uniform translation when applying for business or trademark registration. This name will be your corporate identity in China and will also avoid you later troubles with application procedures. Also, know that certain JVs may need to obtain other specific licenses in order to operate. These licenses can be much more difficult to obtain than the company's original license. For instance, import and sale of consumable goods, trading of certain metals, fuel, rare earths, and pharmaceuticals, all require additional licensing applications. Therefore, you will need a full understanding of the whole process in order to dovetail all the regulatory requirements into your business operations.

Environmental Impact Report

This report is intended to monitor and control manufacturing production processes according to specific environmental norms and standards. The Environmental Protection Bureau will require information about machinery and equipment, the raw materials used, as well as safe and responsible disposal of toxic products. In certain cases, a detailed report on the environmental impact issued by a public, appointed agent is required. For instance, this is the case in the leather or chemical processing business. This may result in a major step to go through as, in the case of a manufacturing company, it could affect the time frame required to get your factory up and running.

Required Documents

Issue of Approval Certificate and Business License

The authorities will issue the Approval Certificate and Business License after assessing the following documents:

From the Investor

- Business License (Certificate of Incorporation which will need to be notarized in the investor's country of origin then

translated into Chinese by a locally registered translation company)
- Bank statement from the relevant bank in the investor's country of origin
- Photocopy of passport of the Legal Representative of the foreign investing company
- Audit Report of the most recent fiscal year for foreign-funded commercial enterprises

From the New Joint Venture

- Feasibility Study Report
- Articles of association
- Environmental Impact Report (Manufacturing companies)
- Documents about the new business (name of the company, business scope, registered capital, business term, lease contract)
- Documents about the Legal Representative (photocopy of passport and passport-sized photos)

Once the certificate of approval will be issued by the local MOFCOM bureau there is a period of 30 days for the registration of the JV with SAIC which will then issue the official business license. After that step, the JV exists as legal entity.

Post-Setup Registration and Filing Procedure

However, the paperwork does not end here. There is still quite a bit to do before you have a fully functioning JV. Be aware that many law firms and consultants do not consider postregistration procedures as part of their business scope when processing customers' applications. Therefore, make sure you search for a company that does, right from the beginning, or ensure that you have this essential component catered for elsewhere because not following correctly on these procedures can lead to government and noncompliance penalties later on.

Below you can see the required documentation necessary to the postregistration procedure:

- Enterprise Code Registration with the Technical Supervision Bureau
- Obtain chops from the Public Security Bureau
- Tax registration and office inspection by the tax bureau
- Registration with the SAFE
- Open RMB and foreign currency bank account
- Open capital bank account
- Customs registration
- Financial registration
- Statistics registration
- Commodity inspection with the Commodity Inspection Bureau
- Injection of capital and Capital Verification Report
- Renewal with SAIC after capital has been injected
- Application for General Tax Payer status

How to Establish a Trading Company (FICE) in China

Key Features

The following criteria must be met before starting the application for establishing a FICE:

- The investor(s) must enjoy a good business reputation.
- They should not have committed any acts in violation of the Chinese law and of administrative rules and regulations.
- They should be able to meet the required ratio between total investment and registered capital.

Foreign Investment Structures in China

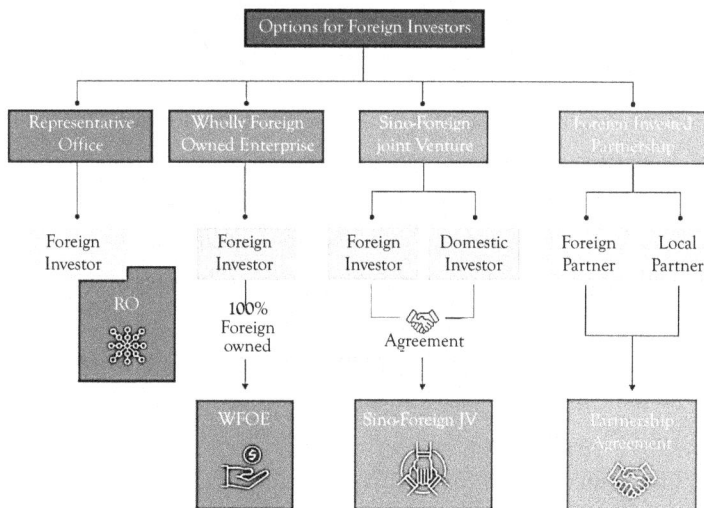

Certain limitations apply to trading companies dealing with specific product categories such as newspapers, books, periodicals, chemical fertilizers, agricultural films, pharmaceutical products, vegetable oil, grains, sugar, and cotton. In case a foreign investor has more than 30 retail stores in China and distributes such products from different suppliers and brands, their share in a retail enterprise is limited to 49 percent.

Mandatory total investment—registered capital ratios	
Total investment (in U.S.$)	Minimum registered capital (in U.S. $)
3 million or below	7/10 of total investment
Above 3 million and below 4.2 million	2.1 million
4.2 million to 10 million	½ of total investment
Above 10 million and below 12.5 million	5 million
12.5 million and below 30 million	2/5 of total investment
Above 30 million and below 36 million	12 million
36 million or above	1/3 of total investment

Required Documents

Note that if documents are not signed by the legal representative, a power of attorney needs to be presented.

The required documents for setting up a FICE are:

- Written application form.
- Feasibility study report signed by all partners/investors.
- Contract, articles of association, and annexes.
- Bank credit certification for each investor, registration certification, and legal representative certification.
- Identity certificate of the investor if an individual.
- Catalogue of import and/or export commodities of the FICE.
- Audit report of the most recent years issued by a registered accounting firm for each investor.
- Evaluation report for state-owned assets that will be invested by the Chinese partner into an equity/cooperative Sino-foreign venture.
- List of members of the board of directors of the FICE and the respective appointment letters from each investor.
- Enterprise name preapproval notice issued by the administrative department for industry and commerce.

- For stores the size of 3,000 m² or larger the FICE must submit a photocopy of the land use rights certification and/or a photocopy of the lease agreement for the store to be established.
- Certificate issued by the competent commerce department stating that the store is in compliance with the provisions regarding urban commercial development.
- Additional documents that might be required by the local administration.

Shortcut Options: Third Jurisdictions as a Gateway to China

Foreign businesses seeking to enter the Chinese market often wonder whether including a third jurisdiction (e.g., Hong Kong or Singapore) in between their home country and China would bring any advantages to their business model. In fact, advantages associated with this type of structure generally include beneficial tax treatment, lower costs, a stable business environment, smooth payment procedures, as well as "verifiable" business partners. Whether these benefits will be materialized depends on multiple factors. In this section I will be focusing on the advantages and disadvantages of using this approach as another way to access the Chinese market. Third jurisdictions, as a gateway option, can be a great platform for foreign businesses seeking to export goods or provide services to mainland China.

Hong Kong

Hong Kong, conveniently located at the southern part of China's prosperous Pearl River Delta region, is regarded by many investors as the ideal gateway to mainland China. In 1997, Hong Kong was returned to China and since then it has kept the status of a Special Administrative Region (SAR). Thanks to the "one country, two systems" policy, it has the unique advantage of being a modern Chinese city and a global trading center continuing to maintain its favored legal and economic structure. Its historic, Western orientation makes it an excellent middle ground between the complexities of mainland China and the way business is conducted in the West. English remains an official language and the region is one of the most liberal market-based economies worldwide. In addition to these benefits, Hong Kong offers world-class infrastructure, low taxes, as well as free flow of capital, labor, and information.

While a large number of multinational companies continue to use Hong Kong as their Asia Pacific headquarters, most foreign businesses usually bypass Hong Kong to enter China directly, especially if they are exporting. There is, however, a variety of reasons for foreign businesses to consider having a legal entity in Hong Kong, depending on the nature of the business, the sector, and the size of the company. For the sake of reference I am providing below some of the most common reasons many foreign businesses choose to set up a Hong Kong company:

- Establishing a holding company to protect the parent company from any negative legal issues that might arise with its business activities in mainland China.
- Benefiting from certain financial and tax systems which include lower corporate tax rates and easier profit repatriation.
- Using a Hong Kong shell company to establish an RO in China (which requires an existing office outside of China). This is a smart strategy and is very popular among foreign entrepreneurs and start-ups without an office in their home country.
- Getting a quick leg up, as you can set up a legal entity in Hong Kong in a very short amount of time (two weeks versus at least three months in mainland China).

The Closer Economic Partnership Arrangement (CEPA) is a bilateral free trade agreement between China and Hong Kong and came into effect in 2004. According to the agreement, China has agreed to eliminate tariffs for all goods of Hong Kong origin and grants preferential treatment to Hong Kong service providers in a number of service sectors. Therefore, foreign companies registered in Hong Kong can benefit from CEPA regulations. More than 40 service sectors fall under CEPA but certain requirements need to be met in order to enjoy preferential treatment. For instance, the company has to be established for a minimum of three years before it is recognized as a Hong Kong-based company. It would be very misleading to claim that foreign companies need to have a link or presence to Hong Kong to be able to successfully do business in mainland China. It is crucial though that companies consider getting further legal advice if they are in doubt about the optimal strategy regarding their specific situation.

Hong Kong's Advantages

Hong Kong is one of the most important international financial centers worldwide. As of 2020, more than 9,000 foreign companies operate in Hong Kong, among them 1,300 from the United States. China is the second largest recipient of FDI in the world. According to the National Bureau of Statistics of China, approximately two-thirds of all the FDI into China came via Hong Kong in 2019. It hosts 142 licensed banks and more than 80 ROs of banks from 40 countries. Supervised by the Hong Kong Monetary Authority and the Securities and Futures Commission, Hong Kong's banking system is very well regulated. Due to the local economy structure, banks based in Hong Kong enjoy a solid international focus, with strengths in project finance and trade. Holding funds in Hong Kong to support or facilitate operations in China enables foreign businesses to enjoy the transparency, freedom, and speed of one of the world's most business-friendly banking systems.

Since there are no foreign exchange restrictions or capital controls, like is the case in mainland China, operating a Hong Kong-based multicurrency trading business is efficient and straightforward. With multicurrency accounts, transactions can be completed in most foreign currencies while telegraphic transfers can be executed on the same day. In addition, there is a broad variety of lending and investment options due to the big number of banks, private equity, and venture capital firms that operate in Hong Kong. Most of these fund providers are familiar with the business environment in China and can offer valuable assistance to foreign enterprises in addition to financing. A major concern of many foreign companies and Chinese exporters is the risk associated with the RMB currency. Many banks in Hong Kong currently offer their customers RMB accounts providing flexibility when making payments to and from China. In fact, the availability of RMB banking is a valuable advantage and makes it easier to negotiate with Chinese customers and business partners. Recent political unrest in Hong Kong, following the enactment of the 2020 Security Law, has naturally raised concerns regarding the special status of Hong Kong and the future of foreign companies operating there. Although this law does not affect businesses and financial activities, the high level of concern the business community has expressed is due to the ambiguity of the law. The law is written vaguely enough that any criticism of the Chinese government or actions that penalize China could potentially violate its terms.

Beneficial Tax Regime

A simple and territorial basis of taxation is operated in Hong Kong whereby tax on profits is imposed only where the transaction has a local source, whereas foreign-sourced income remitted to Hong Kong is not subject to taxation. Therefore, transactions can very well be booked through a Hong Kong company and still not be taxable in Hong Kong. The corporate tax rate is 16.5 percent for transactions originating in Hong Kong, while offshore transactions are not liable to any tax. Salary tax is nothing more than a modified flat tax rate of 15 percent of gross income. In Hong Kong there are no taxes such as capital gain tax, real estate tax, VAT, or sales tax. For instance, dividends received from your China-based company to your Hong Kong corporate account are not taxed in Hong Kong and the remittance to the parent company in your home country is also free of withholding taxes.

Dividends paid by a Chinese company to a Hong Kong entity are liable to a 5 percent withholding tax rate, given that certain conditions are met. Dividends from China to most Western countries are generally subject to a 10 percent dividend withholding tax rate. However, to qualify for reduced tax rates, companies must meet certain requirements set out by the Chinese State Administration of Taxation, in which case the resulting tax rates are among the lowest provided under the Chinese tax system. With 0 percent tax on dividend income and 0 percent withholding tax rate on dividends remitted overseas, Hong Kong is the ideal channel foreign companies can use to repatriate income and profits. The 2006 double taxation agreement between China and Hong Kong, in addition to applying to dividends, reduces the withholding tax rates on royalties and other interests. Moreover, with the right repatriation structures, included in the articles of association of your Chinese company, fees received by your Hong Kong company from your Chinese one are tax free, although there is still a withholding tax of 7 percent, which, again, is less than the 10 percent rate you would have to pay if the shareholder of the China company is not based in Hong Kong.

Hong Kong for International Trading Companies

In this section I discuss the special benefits that Hong Kong offers to international trading companies. In fact, a big number of companies seeking to enter the Chinese market are companies exporting services, goods, and technology to China. Managing and coordinating your international trade business from halfway around the globe can be a costly and particularly laborious process. Differences in currencies, time zones, protocol, and language are only the tip of the iceberg. For many Western companies selling to China, one option is to outsource elements of their international trade by changing the sales location from their home country to Hong Kong which can be achieved through selling directly from the company based in your home country to your Hong Kong subsidiary which then sells to China.

This process works in the following way. First, you establish a Hong Kong limited company, which is a wholly owned subsidiary of the company based in your home country. The Hong Kong subsidiary then buys from the mother company or directly through the company's suppliers to sell to the Chinese buyer, thus invoicing the sale through Hong Kong. The Hong Kong company pays the cost of goods sold either to the mother company or to the supplier and receives payment from the Chinese buyers. All profits are sent back to the Hong Kong company in the form of management fees, as dividends, or simply by cost of goods sold from the mother company. This way, only a small profit amount is recorded in Hong Kong and there are a number of ways to transfer that profit back to your home country in an easy and tax-efficient manner. It is easy to set up this structure using a Hong Kong-based service provider specializing in this sort of arrangements. An added benefit is that, by outsourcing most international trade functions, you can focus your efforts on the key elements of your customer and vendor relationship, such as production, local distribution, and building your network, while leaving the paperwork aspects of these relationships to your service provider.

Singapore

Singapore is China's third largest investor. The city-state of Singapore was founded in 1819 as a British colony. After joining the Malaysian federation in 1963, it separated two years later and became an independent state which subsequently became one of the world's most prosperous economies with powerful international trading links and with per capita GDP equal to that of the leading Western European nations. Strategically located at the center of Asia's major growing markets of China and India and the emerging Asian economies, Singapore offers tremendous opportunities for business growth to Western companies. The country is an international transportation hub with many air and sea trade routes. It is well supported by an excellent financial infrastructure, political stability, English-speaking skilled workforce, a sound infrastructure, and extensive market connectivity. Singapore is ideally positioned to be the gateway to China for global companies and growing Asian businesses. Using a Singapore holding company structure can translate into substantial tax savings for many Western companies. Hong Kong's global and regional standing in finance facilitates the coordination of capital requirements for the region. If the particulars of the 2020 Security Law for Hong Kong that China recently passed end up being strict enough, and reactions from the United States and United Kingdom are strong enough that Hong Kong's standing in the financial markets shrinks significantly, Singapore could become an attractive alternative for regional headquarters. Many aspects of its financial market, from company listings to foreign currency exchange, already rival or surpass Hong Kong. Its political security, efficient infrastructure, quality schools, and other features only add to its attractiveness as a base for regional headquarters. U.S. technology firms in fact already have twice as many regional headquarters in Singapore as in Hong Kong.

For the many years in a row Singapore has been ranked by the World Bank as one of the easiest places to do business in the world. As a leading financial center, Singapore is seeking to become a trading and investment hub for the Chinese Yuan. Many financial analysts regard Singapore as a bridge between Europe, East Asia, and the Middle East. Apart from its key geographical location, Singapore offers the cultural advantages of a multi-ethnic society where over 70 percent of the population is Chinese. Trade between China and ASEAN (Association of South East Asian Nations) has seen a dramatic growth in the last decade with more and more business being done in Chinese RMB instead of dollars. Recently, the Bank of China and the Industrial and Commercial Bank of China were both given full bank licenses in Singapore and were granted permission to open 25 local branches in the city-state. Singapore has become the first country outside China to host RMB clearing accounts. Foreign investors wishing to establish a business in Singapore can choose from a wide range of business structures. Below I am providing a description of the main Singapore business structures available to foreign investors. Private limited companies are the most popular option for doing business in Singapore.

Over the years, Singapore-based companies with their services, products, and capabilities have built up a strong reputation for reliability and quality in China. The expertise that many Singapore companies possess dovetails with the increasing needs of the evolving Chinese economy for modern business solutions. These factors, coupled with Singapore's familiarity with the Chinese culture and language, provide a comparative advantage to Singapore companies wanting to enter China. As exports to the recession-stricken West decline and government spending becomes more responsible, China's focus on boosting domestic consumption and expanding urbanization creates many opportunities. Many Singapore companies whose expertise and strength lie in the service industry will benefit from the gradual liberalization of sectors such as education, health care, and environmental services.

Setting up a company in Singapore is pretty straightforward and fast. It is a very popular option and an alternative to Hong Kong for foreign investors seeking to create an entity before entering the Chinese market. Entrepreneurs starting a business in Singapore can be confident of a fair legal system which protects IPRs. Most foreign entrepreneurs prefer a Singapore LLC to conduct international business although other entity types are also available, such as sole proprietorship, limited liability partnership (LLP), branch company, and RO. The process of establishing a company is done through the Accounting and Regulatory Authority of Singapore (ACRA). The current cost for registering a company with ACRA is S$300.

After the company registration is completed, the company must register for GST (Goods and Sales Tax) in case sales exceed RMB 1 million (U.S.$801,540) per year. Singapore levies a 7 percent of GST in lieu of import duties and VAT. On the other hand, company sales to international customers are GST exempt. Investors who establish a company in Singapore have access to a wide range of double taxation treaties. Singapore has signed such agreements with 62 countries, including China, Japan, Germany, France, the United Kingdom, and Canada.

Private Limited Company

In Singapore, the private limited company is commonly known as "PTE Ltd" company. A private limited company offers investors the flexibility to protect their personal assets from the company's liabilities. There are special tax benefits this particular company structure can benefit from. A PTE Ltd has its own legal identity which is separate from its members: shareholders (who own the company) and directors (who manage the company). Corporation tax is paid by the company on their profits. A PTE Ltd must have less than 50 members. Members have limited liability and are not personally responsible about the losses and debts of the company. This type of structure is subject to tax as a Singapore-based resident entity. The PTE Ltd must appoint a minimum of one director who ordinarily resides in Singapore. This company structure is very similar to the German GmbH.

Branch Office

Foreign companies seeking to set up a place of business or conduct business in Singapore may opt for a branch office. In fact, a Singapore branch is considered an extension of the foreign company and not a distinct legal entity. As a result, it is the mother company of a branch office that is liable for the losses and debts of the branch. The taxation basis for a branch office is the same as that for a resident entity. On the other hand, the branch office is not eligible for incentives and tax exemptions offered to local companies. In addition, the branch must appoint two agents residing permanently in Singapore.

Representative Office

Foreign companies wishing to get a foothold in Singapore may consider to set up an RO as a way to assess the business environment there before deciding to step fully into China or before committing to a more permanent structure. The rules are pretty much the same as in the case of a China-based RO. An RO is not allowed to engage in any commercial or profit-making activities. As such, it is not subject to taxation and, given that it has no legal identity, all liabilities extend to the mother company. A Singapore RO may operate for a maximum period of three years, provided that its status is evaluated and renewed on an annual basis. The RO's activities are supervised by a chief representative, appointed by the mother company.

Sole Proprietorship

A sole proprietorship is a business carried on by an individual. It is usually a one-person operation without the use of a distinct business form. A sole proprietor is personally liable for all obligations and debts of the business. Profit generated by the business is the income of the sole proprietor who is taxed on an individual basis. A sole proprietorship must appoint at least one Singapore-based manager if he or she resides outside of Singapore.

Partnership

A partnership is defined as the relationship between physical persons carrying on business together with a view to a profit. In Singapore a partnership can legally have up to 20 partners. Such a structure does not have a separate legal status. Therefore, the partners are liable for all obligations and debts of the business. Profits are distributed to the partners who, in turn, are taxed on an individual basis. In case all partners reside outside of Singapore, a Singapore-based manager should be appointed.

Limited Partnership

Another popular business structure is the Limited Partnership or "LP," a business organization consisting of one or more general partners and one or more limited partners. In an LP a general or limited partner can either be an individual or a corporation. The legal status of an LP is not separate from that of its partners. An LP cannot sue or be sued or even own property in its own name. A general partner is legally responsible for all obligations and debts of the LP, while a limited partner is only liable up to the amount of their agreed contribution. However, while a general partner can take part in the management of the business, a limited partner cannot. As an LP is not liable to tax at an entity level, each partner is taxed on their share of the income they earn from the LP.

Limited Liability Partnership

An LLP is an interesting business structure in the sense that it combines the operational flexibility of a partnership with the limited liability characteristics of a company. It is a corporate body, capable of suing and be sued, with a legal status separate from that of its partners. It can also own property in its name. Every LLP must have a minimum of two partners. As in the case of the LP, an LLP partner can be either an individual or a company. However, partners are not liable for any obligation of the LLC. Partners are only liable for any individual omission or wrongful act without being liable for any omission or wrongful act of any other LLP partner. Each partner is taxed on their own share of the income they receive from the business activities of the LLP.

Hong Kong and Singapore: Tax Similarities and Differences

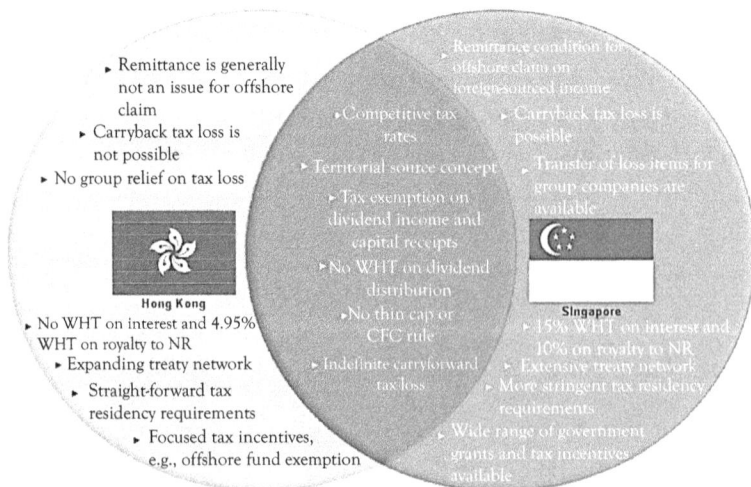

Tax and Accounting

When deciding to set up office in China most companies face a long list of practical issues they need to deal with. Legislation and taxation issues, as well as IPR, hiring employees, conducting due diligence before deciding to commit to a partnership with a local company, or the right choice of location can be cumbersome and time-consuming processes.

Taxation in China is a complex topic because legislation is constantly changing. The State Administration of Taxation (SAT) and the Ministry of Finance (MOF) are the authorities empowered to interpret China's tax laws and regulations. The SAT is responsible for the formulation and coordination of tax policies as well as for the supervision of the work of local tax bureaus established on provincial and municipal levels. On the other hand, the MOF is responsible for the administration of China's national budget and macroeconomic policies. Economic regulations and fiscal policies are also managed by the MOF.

The Chinese current tax system is relatively new. It has only been developed since the 1980s. To tackle unfair competition, Chinese lawmakers passed the Corporate Income Tax Law in 2007 which unified the tax rates for domestic and foreign enterprises. The law took effect back in 2008 and brought China's tax laws more in line with international taxation standards. It unified the two existing tax codes: one for domestic and one for FIEs into one. This represents a radical change in China's tax policy. The Corporate Income Tax Law contains chapters as well as general and supplementary provisions on what constitutes tax incentives, taxable income, withholding taxes, special tax adjustments, and so on.

CIT is a tax on profits. It is calculated against the company's net income in a financial year after deduction of reasonable business expenses and losses and although it is settled on an annual basis, it is often paid quarterly with adjustments refunded or carried forward to the following year. The final calculation is generally based on the year-end audit. Tax planning can be a complicated matter as the Chinese government levies different taxes at different tax rates depending on the business scope and the location of an enterprise. When structuring your China investment careful attention should be paid to income and turnover taxes.

Overview of China's Business Taxes

Overview of tax rates	
Common taxes	Tax rate
Individual income tax • Income on wages and salaries • Production and business income • Others	3%–45% 5%–35% 20%–40%
Enterprise income tax • Income of China-based enterprises • Lower tax rate (e.g., high-tech companies) • China-sourced income of foreign companies without establishment in China • Income of foreign enterprises with establishment in China, when income is not related to the establishment	25% 15% 10% (withholding tax) 10% (withholding tax)
Turnover tax VAT • Sales of goods, import, processing • General VAT taxpayer Tax rates under the VAT reform • Export goods • Transportation services • Other services (e.g., Consulting, IT, Research and development) • Small taxpayer Business tax • Depending on the company's business scope	17% 13% 0% 11% 6% 3% 5% (3%–20%)
Consumption tax • Luxury goods (cosmetics, alcohol, tobacco, etc.)	3%–45%

Who Is Paying What

Foreign taxpayers in China include FIEs (e.g., WFOEs, FICEs, and JVs), individuals (foreign private investors, shareholders), as well as foreign expatriates and foreign independent freelancers.

Foreign-Invested Enterprises (FIEs)

- WFOEs
- FICEs

- Foreign EJVs
- Foreign cooperative JVs

Foreign Enterprises (FE)

- China-sourced income (e.g., interest, royalties, rent)
- Permanent establishment (e.g., WFOE, RO)

Foreign Individuals

- Foreign private investors (e.g., shareholder of a FICE)
- Foreign expatriates working in China (e.g., employees of a WFOE)
- Foreign independent freelancers (e.g., independent lawyer)

Tax Categories

Taxes on Turnover

- VAT
- Consumption tax (CT)
- Business tax (BT)
- Customs tax on exports/imports

Taxes on Income

- Individual Income Tax (IIT)
- Enterprise Income Tax (EIT)

Taxes on Property and Transactions

- Land VAT
- Vehicle and vessel usage tax
- Urban real estate tax
- Stamp tax
- Contractual tax/deed tax

Taxes on Natural Resources

- Land usage tax
- Resource tax

Tax Registration and Declaration

All companies should register with national and local tax bureaus within 30 days after the official establishment of the enterprise. Once they receive approval for the company's tax status, general VAT taxpayers must register with the relevant VAT bureaus for VAT purposes. Companies that are not based in China do not need to register for VAT. ROs shall apply for tax levying.

Annual Tax Declaration/Clearance

EIT: Within the first five months with audited statutory financial statement

There is a 0.05 percent late payment surcharge on delaying tax declaration.

Periodic Tax Declaration Procedures

Monthly: BT, VAT, IIT, and so on
Quarterly: Preapplication of EIT

Other taxes (e.g., land taxes) are due in the second month following a transaction.

In this section we will be focusing on seven types of taxes:

- CIT
- Withholding Tax (WT)
- BT
- VAT
- CT
- IIT
- Customs Duties (CD)

Corporate Income Tax

Since 2008 when the new Corporate Income Law came into effect, tax rates for both domestic and foreign companies were unified. The current income tax rate for all China-based companies is 25 percent. Although settled on an annual basis CIT is often paid quarterly with adjustments either refunded or carried forward to the following year. The final calculation is based on the year-end audit report.

Withholding Tax

WT is a tax levied on overseas enterprises providing services to domestic or foreign China-based businesses. Passive income received by nonresident companies in China (e.g., bonuses, dividends, royalties, rentals, equity investment gains, interests, transfer of property) is also taxable. China has tightened the policies and procedures regarding this form of tax. Nonresident companies with or without establishment in China shall pay tax on their China-based income. The income tax payable on such income shall be withheld at source, meaning that the payer should be the withholding agent. The current WT rate is currently 10 percent (it used to be 20 percent before 2008). If your home country has entered into a double tax treaty with China that includes reduced WT, the foreign party can enjoy reduced tax rates upon approval from the relevant tax bureau.

Tax rate on dividends from tax treaties	
Tax rate	Countries (regions)
0%	Georgia (if the beneficial owner holds directly or indirectly a minimum of 50% of the capital of the enterprise paying the dividends and the total investment amount is no less than U.S.$2.7 million)
5%	Saudi Arabia, Bahrain, Oman, Barbados, Seychelles, FYROM, Croatia, South Africa, Laos, Sudan, Yugoslavia, Jamaica, Slovenia, Mauritius, Mongolia, Kuwait
5%	Venezuela, Georgia (when investment in the company paying the dividends is no less than U.S.$135,000). There will be 10% of gross dividends if the beneficial owner is the direct holder of less than 10% of capital of the company paying the dividends

5%	Singapore, Hong Kong, Trinidad and Tobago, Cuba, Moldova, Ireland, Estonia, Latvia, Lithuania, Iceland, Armenia, Ukraine, Korea, Luxembourg (10% of gross dividends in case the beneficial owner is the direct holder of less than 25% of the capital of the company paying the dividends)
7%	United Arab Emirates
7%	Austria
8%	Egypt, Tunisia, Mexico
10%	Other cases

Value-Added Tax

All enterprises and individuals engaging in the following business activities are required to pay VAT:

- Sale of goods
- Import of goods in China
- Provision of processing, repair, and replacement services

There are two categories of VAT taxpayers: general taxpayers and small-scale taxpayers. Taxpayers with an annual sales volume exceeding the annual sales threshold. Taxpayers must apply to the tax department to be recognized as small scale or general taxpayers. The VAT for general taxpayers is generally 17 percent (13 percent for certain goods) while the current VAT rate for small-scale taxpayers is 3 percent. VAT payable depends on two figures: input VAT and output VAT. Output VAT is that payable on the goods and services sold by a company. Input VAT is that payable on the services or goods bought by a company from another supplier. In fact, the input VAT is used as a credit against the output tax levied on the sale of the goods. The VAT payable is the output VAT for a given period, after deducting the input VAT for the same period. The formula goes as follows:

VAT payable = Output VAT – Input VAT

To resolve the problem of duplicate taxation on services and goods and to support the development of the service industry a pilot project was launched two years ago to replace BT with VAT in the transport and certain service sectors. Shanghai was the first city to implement this pilot project back in 2012. Under Shanghai's current pilot scheme VAT is applied at an 11 percent rate to transport services and at a 6 percent rate to modern services, excluding tangible movable property leasing services.

Business Tax

BT is a form of tax payable against turnover by all individuals and enterprises undertaking the following business activities:

- Provision of taxable services, including transport, communications, construction, insurance, finance, culture, telecommunications, service, and entertainment industries
- Transfer of intangible assets
- Sale of real estate

BT rates vary from 3 percent to 20 percent, depending on the industry. BT also applies to services where either the service provider or the service buyer is located in China, regardless of where the service is being rendered. BT is normally calculated, filed, and paid every month to the local tax bureau. As part of China's current FYP, BT will be replaced by VAT, a transition already under way.

Common Business Tax rates	
Industry	Tax rates (%)
Transportation	3%
Finance and insurance	3%
Servicing agencies	3%
Construction	3%
Culture and sports	3%
Sales of immovable properties	3%
Post and telecommunications	3%
Transfer of intangible assets	3%
Entertainment	5–20%

Consumption Tax

CT applies whenever luxury goods belonging in certain industry sectors are manufactured, imported, or processed in China. Tax rates vary depending on the product category. For instance, a rate of 36 percent is applied against cigars and a 3 percent on motor vehicle tires. The paid tax is directly computed as a cost and therefore cannot be refunded. If your company is processing taxable goods for clients or other companies, you are liable to withhold and pay CTs based on the value of the raw materials and your processing fees. CT should be filed and paid on a monthly basis.

Another form of tax is the stamp taxes which are levied on contracts regarding sales, purchases, construction, processing contracting and engineering projects, transportation of goods, asset leasing, loans, storage and warehousing, transfer of property rights, asset insurance, royalty license, and so on.

CT is levied in five main categories of products:

- Products the overconsumption of which is harmful to the environment, health, and social order, for example, alcohol, tobacco, fireworks, and firecrackers
- Nonnecessities and luxury goods, for example, cosmetics and precious jewelry
- High-end products and high-energy consumption, for example, luxury cars and motorcycles
- Nonreplaceable and nonrenewable petroleum products, for example, diesel oil and gasoline
- Financially significant products, for example, motor vehicle tires

Custom Duties

CD include import and export duty rates. There are two main categories of export duty rates: general tariff rates and preferential tariff rates. General tariff rates apply to goods originating from countries that haven't concluded "most favored nation" trade agreements with China, whereas preferential tariffs apply to imports originating in countries with which China has signed such agreements. CD are computed either on a value basis by applying an applicable rate or on a quantity basis through applying an amount of duty per product unit.

Tax Incentives

There are a number of tax incentives foreign companies can benefit from, provided they meet relevant requirements:

- Encouraged high-tech companies are eligible for reduced income tax rates of 15 percent regardless of the location of such companies in China.
- Qualified advanced technological service companies are eligible for reduced income tax rates of 15 percent in 21 Chinese cities.
- Research and development costs can be deducted from the taxable income by 150 percent of the total amount.
- Existing preferential tax policies with regard to infrastructure investments, forestry, agricultural, fishery, and animal husbandry industries and for those companies established in the western regions of the country have been retained.
- Further tax incentives will be granted to start-up enterprises and companies investing in industrial safety, energy and water saving, and environmental protection.

Additionally, there are tax incentives available to those qualifying companies which employ laid-off or disabled staff, with substantial deductions applied to the wages of the handicapped employees. Three major tax circulars issued in 2008 impact significantly foreign-invested companies which are active in high-tech and other industry sectors. Preferential tax treatment also applies to IC production and assembly businesses as well as software production companies which have been recently established in the western part of China.

General Taxpayer Status

According to the Measures of the Administration of the Qualification Recognition of VAT General Taxpayers which took effect in 2010, taxpayers with an annual sales volume that does not exceed the small-scale taxpayers' level set by the Ministry of Finance and the State Administration of Taxation as well as taxpayers with newly established businesses can apply to the local tax department for recognition as general taxpayers. It is important to know that full general taxpayer status is not automatically granted to wholesalers. Moreover, it is only after a three-month testing period as a general taxpayer under the supervision of a local tax officer that a wholesaler can obtain the status of a fully certified general taxpayer.

Taxable items	Rate
Export of goods	0%
Cereals and edible vegetable oils, heating, cooling, tap water, coal gas, hot air supplying, hot water, liquefied petroleum gas, natural gas, methane gas, coal or charcoal products for household use, newspapers, books, magazines, feeds, agricultural chemicals, chemical fertilizers, dimethyl ether, agricultural machinery and equipment, plastic covering film for farming, forestry, aquatic products, agriculture, products of animal husbandry, electronic publications, audio-visual products, edible salt, etc.	13%
The sale and import of goods other than those listed in the above section, services of processing, repairs, and replacement	17%

VAT Calculation for General Taxpayers

The VAT rate for general taxpayers is 17 percent or 13 percent for certain goods (as you case in the earlier table). For those taxpayers dealing in goods or providing taxable services with different tax rates, the sale amounts for the different tax rates should be accounted for separately. If they fail to do so, the higher tax rate will apply. VAT payable relies on two main figures: input VAT and output VAT. Output VAT is the one payable on the goods and services sold by a company: output VAT $= A \times B$, where A stands for Sales and B for Tax Rate. Input VAT is that payable on the services and goods a company buys from another company (e.g., a supplier). The input VAT is commonly used as credit against the output tax levied on the sale of goods. The VAT payable should be the output VAT for the designated period, after deduction of the input VAT for that period, that is:

VAT payable = Output VAT – Input VAT

Vat Calculation for Small-Scale Taxpayers

Since 2009, the VAT thresholds for those companies that do not qualify for general taxpayer status have been amended. The sales threshold for small-scale taxpayers was reduced from RMB 1 million and RMB 1.8 million to RMB 500,000 and RMB 800,000, respectively. Additionally, nonenterprise units and entities that do not engage in taxable activities are given the possibility to choose whether they will be taxed as small-scale taxpayers while individual taxpayers (natural persons) with a turnover exceeding the threshold can maintain their small-scale taxpayer status. The VAT rate for small-scale taxpayers is currently 3 percent. Given such taxpayers cannot deduct input VAT, the formula goes as follows: VAT payable = Sales Value × Tax Rate (i.e., 3%).

Profit Repatriation

Before distributing and repatriating profits FIEs must complete annual compliance, a process that involves three steps: audit, tax filing, and annual license inspection and renewal. These procedures, apart from being required by law, are also a great opportunity for the company to conduct an internal financial health check. It is important to know that there are slight variations in annual compliance procedures and major considerations among regions and entity types, with the annual compliance for ROs being different from those for WFOEs and JVs. The first thing the company needs to do is to conduct all the audits required by the region where the FIE is based. The list normally includes a tax verification audit, a financial audit, and a foreign exchange audit. All FIEs must submit the annual taxation reporting package to the local tax bureau by the end of May every year. The reporting package is used to verify all the taxes payable, including BT, VAT, CIT, CT, and other taxes based on the audit result.

In case the audited tax figure is lower than the paid tax, the company needs to apply for a tax adjustment for that fiscal year. In the event the audited tax figure is higher than the paid figure, the company needs to pay the balance due to the tax authorities upon submission of the report. After the audit and the tax filing comes the annual license inspection and renewal, also known as "annual cooperative examination," which is jointly conducted by many government departments, including the local office of the Finance Bureau, the Ministry of Commerce, the Tax Bureau, the Administration of Industry and Commerce, the SAFE, the Customs, and the Statistics Bureau to ensure that foreign-invested companies comply with legal requirements.

Once the inspection process has been completed, the company needs to submit a signed annual cooperative examination report, other prescribed financial information, including the report, and the audited financial statements accompanied by other materials (signed and stamped) to the relevant administrative body by the end of June of every year. After submitting the annual audit and completing the tax payment a net profit figure is derived. The planning for declaration of dividends for repatriation and/or reinvestment of profits depends on the current situation of your Chinese company and its parent company abroad. Additionally, repatriation of profits becomes a less cumbersome procedure if the company requires the funds for reinvestment abroad or for return to the shareholders.

Here, it is important to note that not all profits can be repatriated or reinvested because a portion (a minimum of 10 percent for WFOEs) should be placed in a reserve fund account. This sum is treated as part of the owner's equity on the balance sheet. In addition, it is a common practice in China that the investor allocates some of the remainder to a staff bonus welfare fund or an expansion fund, although these are not mandatory for WFOEs. The remaining net profit is then available for redistribution. Following a resolution by the board of the directors, the company needs to submit an application form for the repatriation of funds to the tax bureau, which in turn will authorize the bank to disperse the funds.

Location Options

China is changing fast. The country has a population exceeding 1.4 billion people—nearly one-fifth of the world's population—which is a major pool of potential customers for multinational manufacturers and retailers. Entering such a huge and complex market is particularly challenging mainly because access to updated and geographically detailed data about the country's numerous markets is fairly limited. Updating official population census counts would be a very challenging task. However, new techniques using satellite-collected remote sensing data are a new way of monitoring population growth and expanding urbanization. Also the infamous Social Credit System, put in place a few years ago, is expected to play a big role in population monitoring in the coming years. An important element adding to the existing complexity is the way China's geographic regions are defined. The country is primarily divided into provinces, prefectures, counties, and townships. Chinese cities are composed of different administrative divisions. There are three main levels of cities: municipalities, prefecture-level cities, and county-level cities.

Following years of positive economic growth, China has firmly established itself as the world's manufacturing center but that growth is far from being uniform across the whole country, nor even the eastern part, where most of the intense growth has occurred. The 31 provinces, municipalities, and autonomous regions are classified in terms of economic and urban growth, migrant population, and retail sales. By examining such information, businesses are better placed to evaluate and target regional opportunities for further investigation. For instance, Shandong province has high retail sales rates compared to a relatively small migrant population, which implies an important ratio of permanent residents. These permanent residents may have health care demands, home ownership needs, and school children requiring extracurricular activities and related services. By contrast, migrant workers are traditionally big savers and send their earnings back home. They are not eligible for social services; they usually do not own houses and have a much lower "lifestyle" consumption.

An important fact to consider is that costs in first-tier cities like Shanghai, Beijing, and Guangzhou are rising. As a result, a growing number of foreign entrepreneurs and investors are now seeing smaller, second- or third-tier inland cities as the next great opportunity. For more than three decades the eastern part of the country has been developing rapidly following the government's opening-up policy aimed at encouraging foreign investments and promoting the country's integration into international trade. Those areas have actually been the world's manufacturing hubs for over 30 years and are now at the edge of a structural transformation, boosting the growth of the local services industry and moving up the value chain. In the same way the most advanced parts of the country have already been through this path of transition; the inland and western parts are now receiving growing attention from the national authorities and are attracting increasing amounts of domestic investments and FDIs. These regions, as well as the rural parts of the country, are catching up fast and are quickly overtaking those traditional business centers of the country.

China's Major Cities

As you can see in the later table, amongst the top five fastest growing regions three belong to Northwest China—one to the north and one to the south central area of the country—confirming that the inner regions are catching up really fast and offer tremendous opportunities to foreign businesses. In a similar fashion, second- and third-tier cities located in Central and Western China are becoming more and more attractive to investors due to improving infrastructure, higher growth rates, and lower wages. While China's major first-tier cities have traditionally attracted a great number of new-to-China entrants, these new locations are expected to become the future stage of China's development, with some regions already enjoying a reputation for their appeal to certain industry sectors. The geographic areas given in the table are considered the most attractive with regard to sales, research and development, production, and exporting.

Key Points to Consider When Choosing a Location

With a growing number of Chinese cities developing at an incredible speed, it has become increasingly challenging for Western businesses to sell their services and products. Here you can see a list of points that foreign businesses and entrepreneurs need to consider based on the specific needs and goals of their business.

Busines activity	City profile	Cities highlighted
Sales (Local sales)	Higher than avaerage disposable income strong retail sales Good retail infrastructure Lower costs Access to seaports	Chengdu, Dalian, Dongguan, Foshan, Hangzhou, qingdao, Suzhou, Tianjio
Overall domestic (Local production for domestic markets)	Good logistics network Low labour costs Comparatively low energy costs Preferential government policies	Changsha, Chengdu, Dongguan, Hangzhou, Nanjing, Ningho, Shenyang, Suzhou, Tianjin, Wuhan, Xiamen, Zhengzhou
Overall domestic (Local production for export markets)	Easy access to seaports strong concentration of multinational manufacturers Large pool of educated workers Good manufacturing infrastructure and facilities Reliable energy an transportation infrastructure	Dalian, Dongguan, Foshan, Hangzhou, Ningbo, Qingdao, Quanzhou, Suzhou, Tianjin, Wuxi, Xiamen
Research and development (R&D)	Large pool of university educated workers Reputable universities and science and technology facilities High government spending on science and education Concentration of high technology development zones	Changsha, Chengdu, Hangzhou, Jinan, Nanjiog, Suzhou, Tianjin, Whan, Xi'an

Size of the Market

- Population size and growth rate
- Existing customers
- Disposable income

Knowing which cities are on the rise and currently offer the most attractive opportunities for Western businesses is the first step to this process. First-tier cities (Shanghai, Beijing, etc.) are already saturated for many products. Second- or third-tier cities should therefore be seriously considered.

Ease of Bureaucracy

- Time to establish the company/get licenses
- Support services

Going through bureaucracy and administration procedures is traditionally one of the biggest challenges that foreign businesses have to go through when entering the Chinese market. Certain cities will be more experienced than others when it comes to dealing with foreign businesses. These cities generally provide better private and public support services, such as consultants, chambers of commerce, accountants, and lawyers.

Access to Logistics

- Availability of adequate warehousing facilities
- Proximity to ports and airports

Although China's logistics infrastructure is developing very fast, getting products around the country is still time consuming. Knowing which cities are most accessible from ports and offer suitable warehousing facilities will save you money and time in the long term.

Climate

- Suitability of temperature and humidity

Especially for companies providing temperature- or humidity-sensitive products, such as pharmaceuticals or foodstuffs, it is essential to search carefully which cities in China are the most appropriate for their products.

Availability of Resources

- Human resources
- Raw materials

Being close to raw materials and skilled workforce will offer a competitive advantage to those companies that are not merely looking to sell in China but also to produce.

Costs

- HR costs
- Utilities costs
- Office or factory space rent

Costs are rising across China and especially in cities like Shanghai, Beijing, and Shenzhen. For those businesses whose production is resource intensive, it is always worth looking around to find the most suitable and cost-efficient location.

Incentives

- Lower rent
- Tax benefits

Tax benefits are not as prolific as they used to be 10 or 20 years ago but they are still available as part of the government's efforts to support certain policy directives (e.g., to encourage foreign investors to go west or north) or to encourage high-tech companies to set up in developing areas of the country.

Human Resources

In the Chinese labor market, demand for qualified and talented workforce exceeds supply. Although there are an increasing number of Chinese university students available to hire, local graduates are often unsuitable for positions in foreign companies due to a lack of English language skills, soft skills, and working experience. Labor shortage can be a problem for foreign companies entering the Chinese market and besides a limited number of skilled workers there is also a high employee turnover rate, meaning that the big challenge for foreign companies is not only to find talent but also to retain it. Strategies for attracting and keeping employees that usually work outside China to bring results within China are pretty common. It is important to develop an adequate HR strategy which takes cultural differences into account. Talents have several employment options in China and designing a clear employment brand is a valuable advantage when competing with other companies for skilled workforce. Hence, it is necessary to develop a strong brand as an employer—especially for larger companies—a brand that will promote the company's unique selling points to potential employees and reflect its corporate culture. For this reason, corporate values need to be promoted both internally and externally.

Contrary to what many foreign firms are used to, it is very common, even for businesses, to be inundated with applications for every advertised position. It is a widespread practice for most Chinese applicants to send blindly tons of generally formulated job applications to various positions at numerous companies. Moreover, filtering out the most suitable candidates and verifying information contained in the applicants' resumes can be a very hard task, especially for businesses that are not used to handle such a large volume of applications. After scanning and preselecting candidates, it is recommended to have a short phone interview with them to test their level of English.

Also, considering the steadily growing salary expectations in China, it is always useful to ask for the applicant's anticipated wage. This is a common question in China and bringing it up right from the start will save you a lot of time and will make selecting suitable personnel much easier. It should also be noted that compensation data from previous employers tends to be exaggerated.

For businesses finding it difficult to manage big numbers of applications it is recommended to introduce an online recruitment system, already used by many large American and European companies. There are various local companies specializing in this field and can be consulted for help. China's Labor Law is strict and very protective of employee rights, as can be observed in strict stipulations on employment contracts, probation periods, contract termination, or social assurance contributions.

Personal Interview

In a personal interview the candidate should be treated as respectfully as a business partner. They should not wait unnecessarily long. As a sign of courtesy it is common to hand the candidate a business card with both hands and offer a drink. Considering the shortage of talents in many cases the purpose of an interview is not only to get to know the candidate but also to advertise the position. Highly qualified and sought-after candidates are offered many opportunities and therefore need to be convinced first.

For a foreign company to be able to hire the most promising candidates, they should take into consideration their needs and wants. Promotion opportunities, social benefits, and less tangible factors such as the working atmosphere can be more important for Chinese employees than compensation packages. The interview includes very similar questions to the ones used by Western companies. It is advisable to check the frequency of job changes and to ask candidates for which reasons they left former employers. This can be an indicator of how long an executive candidate is likely to stay.

Hiring Expats

For certain positions Western firms might feel more comfortable to hire expatriates. Often, talents are imported due to lack of suitable local candidates. The number of foreign professionals coming to China from all parts of the world is continually increasing. In larger companies exchange programs are organized in which Western employees stay temporarily in China for projects lasting from three months up to one year. These practices become increasingly popular. Employing expatriates presents advantages and disadvantages.

Some of the advantages include:

- Knowledge of the organization, its corporate culture, and how it functions, especially how the job function fits into the company as a whole. This obviously applies to more experienced employees but even younger ones usually understand the company culture better than most Chinese employees would, due to cultural differences.
- The management skills and the educational level of Western employees are usually more suitable to the needs of Western companies; especially in terms of soft skills, such employees have a significant advantage over their Chinese counterparts.

Disadvantages include:

- The cost of hiring expats is considerably higher. The salary of locally hired managers might amount to only 20 percent of the average wage of an expat in a similar position.
- Few expats have the required Mandarin skills to fully manage operations in Chinese. They usually rely on the assistance of local employees.
- Expats have a lack of understanding of the local culture, which makes communication with Chinese employees and relationships with local business partners more difficult.

In fact, workers possessing a unique skill set are those who are Chinese native speakers but have studied or worked abroad for long periods of time. These individuals are more flexible with both cultures and are fluent in both English and Chinese. Another plus is that they are usually demanding lower compensation packages than their Western counterparts.

Contracts

The great majority of employees hired in the private sector are normally given fixed-term contracts. A fixed-term contract can be of any time length but can only be renewed once. On the second renewal the contract becomes an open-term contract which is very hard to terminate. Other types of contracts include employment contracts and part-time contracts, used in limited circumstances.

Dispatch of employees, also known as "secondment," is a very common hiring practice in China. In this situation, the employer pays an HR agency to be in charge of hiring employees. ROs are not allowed to hire staff directly. Therefore, Chinese staff can only be outsourced or "seconded" from a local employment agency. FESCO is the most commonly used term to describe secondment agencies. This is a generic term and is used by many local HR companies all over China.

Following the 1994 unsuccessfully implemented China's Labor Law, the Labor Contract Law of the People's Republic of China came into effect in 2008. The aim of that law was to improve employment relationships and to clarify rights and obligations between employers and employees. According to these regulations employers are liable for damages caused by invalid labor contracts, lack of mandatory minimum content in this type of contracts, or failure to issue employment termination certification. All labor contracts must be in written form. A written contract must be signed by both parties for the employment relationship to be officially established. In case the employer fails to enter into a written contract with an employee for a period of more than 1 month, but less than 12 months, the employer must pay the employee twice the salary for every month they worked without a written contract. If there is no written contract for a period longer than 12 months the contract is considered an open-term contract.

Probation Period

The parties can agree on one probation period only that cannot be extended. The law requires that employers pay their employees at least 80 percent of their contractual salaries, an amount which cannot be lower than the minimum wage. The maximum probation period is always based on the contract terms. In case the employer fails to comply with the statutory probation period, they will need to pay the compensation following the salary standard applicable to the employee after the probation period.

Tax rates for wages	
Working period	Probation period
<3 months	No probation period
3 months to 1 year	A maximum of 1 month
1–2 years	A maximum of 2 months
2–3 years	A maximum of 3 months
>3 years	A maximum of 6 months

Employers are obliged to pay employee salaries in accordance with the national regulations in the employment contract, in full and on time. Regarding noncompetition clauses, be aware that they are legally binding only when they are concerning higher management personnel, employees with access to confidential information, or leading engineers. Noncompetition clauses are valid for a maximum of two years. During this period the employee is not permitted to work for competitors or to set up a competing company. In order to maintain a noncompetition clause, the employer has to pay the employee a decent monthly compensation. It is always advisable to ask the local authorities for further details because regulations vary among provinces. Apart from the probation period, employees can terminate their employment contract with a 30-day cancellation period. Reasons for employee dismissal are strictly regulated by the law. It is important to know that in China it is generally difficult to dismiss employees whose employment contract has not expired.

Employee Handbook

According to the Chinese Labor Law, every company based in China is required to have an employee handbook to protect employees' rights and specify their obligations. It is a critical piece of documentation because it explains in a concise, direct, and detailed manner the company rules and the degree of severity for various infringements. All rules and regulations stipulated in this handbook are considered legally binding in court labor disputes.

An employee handbook is generally aimed to:

- Set out the framework for a company to manage their employee relations.
- Prevent possible misunderstandings with employees.
- Be used as written evidence in legal labor disputes.

Drafting an effective employee handbook right from the beginning is crucial and it is recommended to consult a legal expert. A mistake many companies make is that they do not make their employee handbook detailed enough, which usually results in negative, and often costly, consequences for the employer. For example, if an employee is suing the company for wrongful termination and the employer is unable to prove that the employee was informed, based on the employee handbook that the behavior that led to their dismissal was prohibited, the employee is very likely to win the lawsuit, which might end up being very costly for the company. For the handbook to be an effective tool, employees should be asked to sign it before they start working in the company in order to prove that they have knowledge of its content.

Compensation

Historically low costs for China's huge labor force have been rising frenetically in recent years. The labor supply of certain types of workers, such as skilled labor in inland provinces, and worker retention are also major issues that employers are facing today. Minimum wages vary by province, city, and district. For instance, Shenzhen has the country's highest monthly minimum wage for such workers (RMB 1,800/month) while Beijing has the highest hourly minimum wage (RMB 24/hour). The standard work week in China is 40 hours while overtime compensations are rather steep: 150 percent of basic hourly salary for weekdays, 200 percent for weekends, and 300 percent for public holidays, based on the standard work hour system. Comprehensive work hour systems and nonfixed hour systems are also available but require government approval. As an annual bonus most companies in China must pay 13 months of salary, adding an extra month of salary around Chinese New Year (January/February). Additionally, personal allowances such as monthly cell phone allowance are also common.

Minimum wages across China 2020

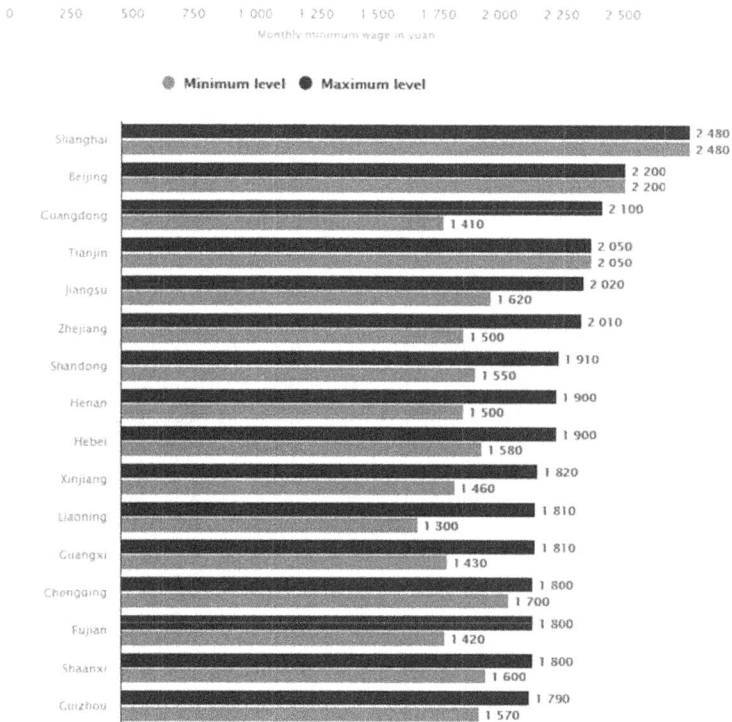

Source: China's Ministry of Human Resources and Social Security

Values are based on current minimum wage levels within each provincial municipality.

Withholding and Paying Individual Income Tax (IIT)

IIT is withheld by the employer from salaries and is paid monthly to the tax authorities, within 15 days from the end of each month. Income from wages is taxed based on progressive rates, ranging from 3 percent to 45 percent of monthly taxable income.

Individual Income Tax Rates and Deductions		
Monthly Taxable Income (RMB)*	Tax Rate	Deduction (RMB)
1,500 or less	3%	0
1,500 < TI ≤ 4,500	10%	105
4,500 < TI ≤ 9,000	20%	555
9,000 < TI ≤ 35,000	25%	1,005
35,000 < TI ≤ 55,000	30%	2,775
55,000 < TI ≤ 80,000	35%	5,505
> 80,000	45%	13,505

*Average rates. Tax rates can change and vary depending on location.

China Residence and IIT Income Source Applicability Timeline

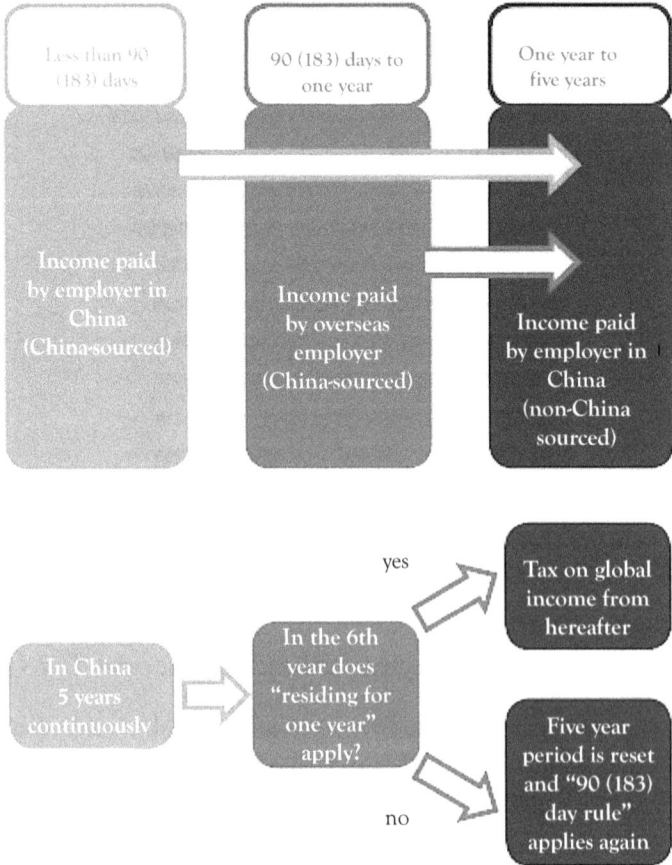

As already mentioned, if an individual is paid by a China-based entity, any income derived from China-based work is taxable. For non-China-sourced income or wages paid by overseas employers, tax obligations normally depend on the period of time an expat employee spends in China.

Contributing to Social Insurance Funds

Social insurance, also known as "social welfare" or "mandatory benefit," payments are mandatory contributions to government-run funds which are made by both the employer and the employee (whose contribution the employing company is responsible for withholding each month). While employees must also contribute to a number of social insurance funds, the portion contributed by the employer is higher than the one contributed by the employee. Moreover, social security payments typically add an extra cost of approximately 30 percent to 40 percent of an employee's monthly salary. Mandatory contribution rates are set by local governments while exact calculations of social security payments are rather complicated. In fact, percentages do not technically depend on the employee's monthly salary but on a theoretical basic salary which is calculated based on a given formula.

There are five main social security funds: pension, unemployment, maternity, medical, and occupational injury fund. Additionally, there is a

Social Security Fund Contributions		
Fund	Approximate Contribution (% of employee's monthly salary)	
	Employee	Employer
Pension	8%[1]	10-22%[2]
Unemployment	0.1-1%	0.2-2%
Medical	2%[2]	7-12%[2]
Occupational injury	N/A	0.4-3%[3]
Maternity	N/A	0-1%
Housing Fund	Normally matched with emplyer	7-13%
Total	10.1%+	24.6-53.0%

[1] *Uniform nationwide*
[2] *Much lower in some cities*
[3] *Also depends on the degree of danger during work*

mandatory housing fund which is not strictly considered a type of social welfare but is generally included within the social security scope because the contributions are mandatory, coming from both the employer and the employee. When the employee purchases a house, the money in the housing fund can be used to pay the initial down-payment on the house or to pay back later the loan to the bank. In 2011 the Chinese government stated that foreign employees are also included in the social insurance system at the same rates as Chinese employees (apart from housing fund). However, implementation varies among regions.

Intellectual Property Rights Protection

IPR infringement is a big issue—and a huge industry—with a long history in China. While the country has been trying to improve its IPR protection laws, especially after joining the WTO in 2001, enforcement remains weak. Nearly all large multinational companies have experienced piracy of their products. Of particular concern is piracy of such products as chemicals and pharmaceuticals which puts public safety at risk. The reason enforcement still remains weak is that the rule of law is shallowly rooted in China. Another important reason is that piracy of big brands is a key source of income in many parts of the country.

Intellectual property has always been an emotive issue and a big concern for all foreign companies and investors operating in China. Considering that the enforcement of IP laws and regulations is not very satisfactory at present, it is crucial for foreign investors to know how to protect their IPR before any infringement occurs. For instance, in the context of a JV, you may be bringing important IP into the business as a resource and therefore you will need to be very careful to protect it, as in a JV case it is no longer your exclusive asset but an asset shared with your Chinese partner, who should be as interested in protecting the IP rights as you are. If the IPRs of your business are vital to your international or China financial interests you may need to assess whether you wish to introduce your technology to China at all. An alternative is to try to assess the amount of time you have with your IP as part of your marketing strategy and work out how much time you are likely to have a free range before plagiarists start eroding the market share.

At the same time, it is equally important to weigh the actual damage against the cost of litigation. Lawyers are costly and emotions might lead you to concentrate more on the litigation than the case actually seems to warrant. It is always wise not to overstate the damage caused to your company in case you actually get ripped off. Try to stay pragmatic when dealing with it. Despite comments to the contrary, Chinese courts are improving in upholding claims of trademark infringement and plagiarism. It is also noteworthy that the great majority of such infringements in China are between Chinese firms. Foreign brands are far from being the only targets. The most valuable brands in the Chinese market are Chinese as mass sales of foreign products are still fairly limited in China. Courts can and do uphold claims by foreign companies where evidence is properly introduced and in order. The problem does not come from the judiciary, although they are not perfect either. The main weakness is enforcement, that is, failure to stop the infringement once a judgment in the foreign company's favor has been awarded. Challenges faced by foreign firms include lack of government support, rewards outweighing the risks for many IP infringers, and growing sophistication—and internationalization—of many piracy operations. Most likely, China's IPR infringement industries will most likely die down with economic growth but I believe that the most efficient way of improving enforcement will come when a larger number of Chinese companies begin to fight in order to protect their own IPRs.

Trademarks and Patents

Many companies believe that because they have already registered their trademark in their home countries, it is automatically covered in China. As China is signatory to all the international protocols drawn up by the international community with regard to the registration and protection of international intellectual property, it follows the same system as most other nations. This includes registration of your company's trademark. If your trademark has been registered under the Madrid protocol, you will be able to apply for extended protection in China. After the Trademark Office in China examines your application, you will most likely receive a Registration Certificate of the Trademark. However, do bear in mind this is not always the case. Your application for extended protection may sometimes be rejected on grounds such as similarity with other registered trademarks belonging in the same subclass while the process for review usually takes at least two years.

International recognition can only be granted provided that the trademark has previously been registered in five other jurisdictions—thus proving its international status—in which case it is considered as an "internationally recognized brand," which, again, is debatable and subject to legal interpretation. However, for practical purposes, even if your company has secured international protection, it is still recommended to register in China as local courts may have difficulty recognizing international protocols if they are not used to them, a process that is both costly and time consuming in terms of legal fees needed to educate the court and provide evidence of the significance of such protocols and China's adherence to them. In any event, trademark registration in China is inexpensive and should be undertaken as a matter of proactivity and good business sense.

Patent infringements are becoming more and more common, and combating this phenomenon is a major challenge for all foreign companies operating in China. When you come to China it is important to consider how to ensure that your competitors will not pirate your key technologies. Patent application should be the first step while careful drafting of the application will help the patent to be approved by the patent authority without too many changes, so that you can enjoy the broadest possible protection allowed by the law. In many patent lawsuits, the patentee ends up losing the case because of the bad wording of the claims. It is therefore very important to find a professional and reliable firm to be in charge of your patent application. There are various patent categories. Most patents are classified into utilities models, inventions, and designs according to the Chinese Patent Law. The patent application fees usually vary, for both initial registration and renewal, depending on the specific application and the category they fall into. The period of validity for invention patents is 20 years while for utility models or design 10 years. Unlike trademarks, once the validity period of a patent has expired, it cannot be renewed.

As mentioned earlier, China is signatory to many international protocols when it comes to the registration of patents and trademarks. However, there is a hole in the registration procedure for patents, requiring that they are registered and placed on public file for assessment before the patent is recognized as intellectual property of a specific firm. This means that certain individuals scan such registrations with the intention to steal designs and then they immediately get into production even when your patent pending process is still ongoing. Bear in mind that this is not a China issue but a weakness in the international protocol of registrations that needs to be addressed to protect expensive R&D and inventions from being used on the cheap by not very scrupulous businesses.

Domain Names

With the exponential expansion of the Internet, an increasing number of people have realized the importance of domain names. Companies usually register their trademark or their enterprise name as their domain name. A good ".cn" domain name will be very useful for marketing. Domain name registration follows the "first come, first served" principle. It is imperative to register the trademark and/or enterprise name before it is hijacked by third parties. A simple research of your logo or company name on the Internet will show the importance of securing a domain name. The annual registration fees for such a domain name are fairly low.

Trade Secrets

"Trade secrets" is a broad concept and it may include all the information and documents that bring financial benefits to the company and that should be protected. Such "secrets" typically include design, production methods, client information, procedures, programs, software, and so on. Trade secrets should be protected not only from competitors but also from key personnel. In case you find yourself in a position of negotiation with potential local partners (e.g., JV setup or a contract) and you need to disclose part of your trade secrets, make sure you sign a confidentiality agreement with the other parties and show them that you are sharing a trade secret.

Regarding key personnel who are in charge of trade secrets, a confidentiality agreement and often a noncompetition agreement are also recommended. Since noncompetition agreements fall within the scope of the local labor law, the company needs to make sure that all the clauses contained in this agreement are in compliance with the current employment laws. It can be very useful if your company can have a person who is in charge of all IPR-related matters, such as building and keeping files, monitoring the IP status, and coordinating with external IP counsels.

It is always best to educate your employees so that they improve their IP consciousness, especially the sales personnel who are most familiar with the local market and the distribution of fake products. Effective communication with your customers will also help to find signs of infringement. IPRs are a sensitive area especially when it comes to JVs because as a foreign investor you will most likely need to share sensitive information with your prospective partner before contracts are signed. Therefore, you will need to register your IP in China immediately and let the JV use the IPRs only under license. Alternatively, you can register the IP as "mutual IP," making sure to specify who is to become the owner when cooperation between the partners is terminated and who will be the owner of the developed IP during the period of JV cooperation. Another use of a company's IP is that it can be used as a capital contribution to a JV, instead of cash contribution. This is an option for foreign companies although it is often not very favorable to do so because a trademark must be already registered in China. Otherwise IP used in this way has to be already patented. Once the IPRs have been secured, they must be transferred to the JV, in which case your parent company will have to be licensed by the JV to use what was formerly its own intellectual property. Some companies choose to license their IP rights to the JV and receive loyalties.

Due Diligence

Daily operations in China, usually thousands of miles away from a foreign company's headquarters, are shielded by a thick language barrier and a business culture that places little value on contracts and accepts less transparent transactions. Widespread allegations of financial and operational irregularities against Chinese companies have caught the attention of many Western media, encouraging those engaging in business transactions with Chinese companies to take a closer look at the way these firms are being run. For Western companies considering mergers and acquisitions or other types of investment in Chinese companies, thorough due diligence on target companies is necessary.

For those with China-based FIEs the most appropriate tools for minimizing opportunities for fraud is to conduct thorough due diligence on potential distributors, suppliers, or other partners as well as effective, internal control systems with routine internal audits. Do bear in mind that Western approaches to internal control and due diligence are far from being comprehensive in China; these processes must be tailored to the Chinese business context. In the broad sense, due diligence is a thorough review of a company aimed at uncovering any lack of compliance, fraud, or other issues. Due diligence procedures are normally split into financial, legal, and operational due diligence. A due diligence checklist in China generally includes the same items used elsewhere:

- Financial documents: current financial statements, annual audits, loans, tax returns, and so on.
- Legal documents: company establishment documents, government approval documents, licenses, and so on.
- Documentation for real estate and land use rights. (In China, the land is exclusively owned by the state; an individual can only buy land use rights.)
- Documentation for IPRs and hard assets.
- Major contracts, distribution records, and so on.

- HR administration documents.
- Litigation history and outstanding litigation.

Due diligence can uncover a wide variety of internal problems, from a company totally misrepresenting its financial standing to minor accounting errors that might be coming from a lack of knowledge or misguided actions. Some common points that need careful attention when it comes to conducting financial due diligence in China include:

- Two or more sets of bank accounts
  It is a fairly common practice that companies keep two or more sets of bank accounts to avoid tax. However, this practice is also used to cover up inappropriate financial behavior.
- "Off the books" revenue
  Underreporting of accounts receivable is often used to reduce taxable income by hiding sales.
- Employees paid "off the books"
  Sometimes, employees are paid off the books as a way to reduce expenses and to avoid paying labor taxes. This can very likely result in high liabilities related to social security and IIT.
- Phantom assets and contracts
  The assets lists on the books are sometimes either understated or overstated. Certain assets are often "mixed" with those of the shareholders.

Additionally, strong internal control systems as well as periodic internal control audits are paramount to prevent fraud when running a business in China. Common types of fraud that can be found across departments include:

Payroll

- Discrepancy between payroll payments and contract salaries
- Deliberate unauthorized use of welfare benefits

- Nonexistent employees—also known as "ghost employees"—whose salary is often deposited into the bank account of another employee

Supply Chain

- Poor inventory control
- Fake VAT invoices
- Improper disposal of scrap
- Purchasing of overpriced raw materials usually due to inappropriate agreement or relationship between supplier and staff

Sales

- Payment of unauthorized sales commissions to friends or employees
- Sales of goods below cost due to inappropriate agreement or relationship between purchaser and staff
- Lack of competitive bidding process

A key feature of the Chinese legal system is the use of official company chops as a way to legally authorize documentation (usually in place of a signature). This actually represents great opportunity for fraud. Therefore, chops should not all be held by one person and the company should take steps to ensure that chops are not misused. Always depending on their business scope a company can hold any number of chops, each for a different purpose and used on various types of official documentation, for example, company chop, contract chop, financial chop, invoice chop, and customs chop. An internal audit control ordered directly by the head-quarters is the best way to evaluate the effectiveness of internal control systems in order to prevent fraud in a China-based entity. The reason is that an internal audit engaged by the China-based entity itself reports to that entity only. In case fraud is discovered at the local level it may not be reported to the headquarters.

Final Thoughts

China's focus on quality projects is expected to lead to more transparency and a reduction in the risks involved. Consultancies are, in this regard, well placed to conduct due diligence of opportunities to help their clients avoid "buying wrong" or "buying expensive" when making investments and well suited to help their clients navigate differing tax and regulatory requirements. The focus now is mostly on assessing each project on its individual merits, while being mindful of the goal of spreading prosperity and inclusiveness.

Laozhu, a well-known philosopher and poet of Ancient China, famously said that "a journey of a thousand miles begins with a single step." I do hope that this book has provided you with sufficient information so that you now feel more ready to start planning your China market entry. Entering the Chinese market—as any other market—requires long-term planning and experience. Developing the right strategy according to the specific needs of your business will bring you closer to success and will save you a great deal of time and financial resources. Having a solid team on the ground, local advisors, as well as a solid network of local and foreign contacts will help you navigate China's particularly chaotic business environment during pre-entry, execution, and growth of your business in China.

The Chinese market has often been described as a "dog fight" while many Western business people with long China experience go farther and define it as the world's most competitive market. An additional challenge Western companies face in China is the full-throttle pace of change in the business environment. It is very likely that many Western companies will find most of their global rivals in China. Meanwhile, local competitors are leaping ahead in sophistication, quality, and speed. Several international companies often find themselves squeezed by domestic players adept at replicating their best product features while at the same time slashing prices. The key survival skills for China are flexibility, innovation, speed, a great marketing strategy, as well as careful and constant tracking of consumer preferences. Taking smart risks and adapting to the Chinese market and local business environment while seizing emerging opportunities as they arise is part of the China game.

Going Forward: Decision-Making Flowchart

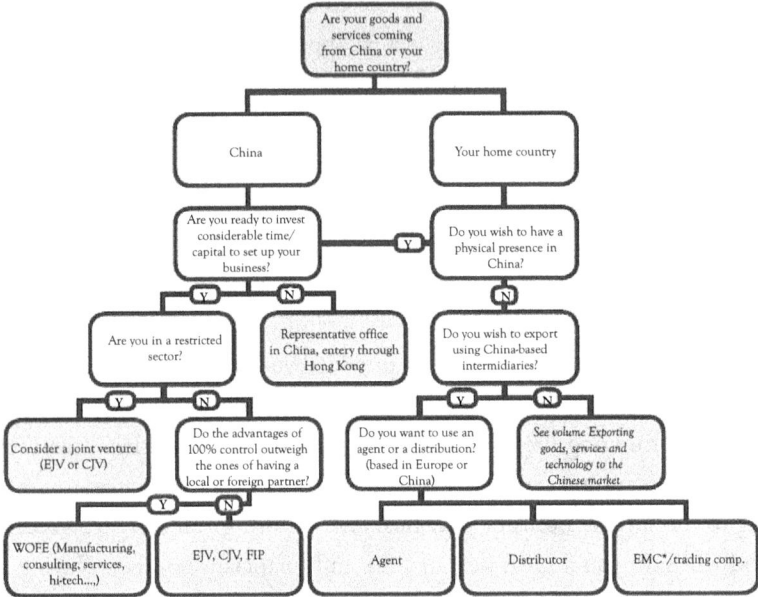

EMC: *Export Management Consultant*

Note: In all the cases, creating an entity/holding company in Hong Kong may have some value and using online platforms as a sales channel may be a viable strategy.

Useful Links

Chinese Government Bodies

- Ministry of Commerce Invest in China: information on foreign investment for domestic enterprises and foreign investors (English and Chinese)
  http://fdi.gov.cn
- Ministry of Commerce MOFCOM (English and Chinese)
  http://mofcom.gov.cn
- People's Republic of China General Customs Administration (Chinese)
  http://customs.gov.cn
- People's Republic of China State Administration of Foreign Exchange (SAFE; English and Chinese)
  http://safe.gov.cn
- State Administration of Taxation (Chinese)
  http://chinatax.gov.cn
- Chinese Ministry of Finance (Chinese)
  http://mof.gov.cn
- Beijing Foreign Economic and Trade Commission (English and Chinese)
  http://tpbjc.gov.cn
- Beijing Foreign Investment Service Centre (English and Chinese)
  http://bfisc.com
- National Audit Office of the People's Republic of China (English and Chinese)
  http://cnao.gov.cn

Chambers of Commerce and Business Councils

- Australian Embassy in Beijing
  http://austemb.org.cn

- American Embassy in Beijing
  http://usembassy-china.org.cn
- British Embassy in Beijing
  http://britishembassy.org.cn/english/index.shtml
- Canadian Embassy in Beijing
  http://beijing.gc.ca/
- German Embassy in Beijing
  http://deutschebotschaft-china.org/de/home/index.html
- French Embassy in Beijing
  http://ambafrance-cn.org
- Italian Embassy in Beijing
  http://italianembassy.org.cn
- Australian Consulate General in Shanghai
  http://china.embassy.gov.au/shanghai/eindex.html
- American Consulate General in Shanghai
  http://usembassy-china.org.cn/shanghai
- British Consulate General in Shanghai
  http://britishembassy.org.cn/english/shanghai/bcgs.shtml

Accounting and Auditing in China

- State Administration of Taxation (Chinese)
  http://chinatax.gov.cn
- Beijing Institute of Certified Public Accountants (Chinese)
  http://bicpa.org.cn
- Chinese Securities and Regulatory Commission (English and Chinese)
  http://csrc.gov.cn
- Chinese Institute of Certified Public Accountants (English and Chinese)
  http://cicpa.org.cn
- Information about accounting terms and regulations in China (English and Chinese)
  http://accgo.com

Local Business Environment in China

- China business and information link (English)
  http://cbw.com
- China business news (English)
  http://c-biz.org
- Economic news, market analysis, and statistical information about China (English and Chinese)
  http://cei.gov.cn
- Chinese National Bureau of Statistics (Chinese)
  http://chinastatistics.com
- Database of recent updates to Chinese law (Chinese)
  http://law-lib.com/law
- TDC is the global marketing arm and service hub for Hong Kong-based manufacturers, traders, and service exporters (English)
  http://tdctrade.com

About the Author

Danai Krokou was born in Corfu, a Greek island in the Ionian Sea. She left her hometown at age 17 to study and work in numerous countries around the world. She is an international business development consultant, Chinese market investment specialist and passionate polyglot. She has lived and worked in France, the United Kingdom, Spain, Austria, Greece, Hong Kong and China. She studied business, foreign languages, and international politics. She is fluent in a handful of languages including Mandarin Chinese. She started her first business at age 25 in Shanghai, PRC. She is also the author of *The Chinese e-Merging* and *Trading with China,* published by BEP.

For more information visit: www.danaikrokou.com

Index

OTHER TITLES IN THE
INTERNATIONAL BUSINESS COLLECTION

Tamer Cavusgil, Georgia State, Michael Czinkota, Georgetown, and Gary Knight, Willamette University, Editors

- *Creative Solutions to Global Business Negotiations, Third Edition* by Claude Cellich
- *Exporting* by Laurent Houlier and John Blaskey
- *Global Trade Strategies* by Michel Borgeon and Claude Cellich
- *Doing Business in Germany* by Andra Riemhofer
- *Major Business and Technology Trends Shaping the Contemporary World* by Hamid Yeganeh
- *Doing Business in the United States* by Anatoly Zhuplev, Matthew Stefl and Andrew Rohm
- *Globalization Alternatives* by Joseph Mark Munoz
- *Major Sociocultural Trends Shaping the Contemporary World* by K.H. Yeganeh
- *Doing Business in Russia, Volume II* by Anatoly Zhuplev
- *As I See It'* by Michael R. Czinkota
- *Creative Solutions to Global Business Negotiations, Second Edition* by Claude Cellich and Subhash Jain
- *Doing Business in Russia, Volume I* by Anatoly Zhuplev
- *In Search for the Soul of International Business* by Michael R. Czinkota
- *Entering the Chinese e-Merging Market* by Danai Krokou

Announcing the Business Expert Press Digital Library

Concise e-books business students need for classroom and research

This book can also be purchased in an e-book collection by your library as

- a one-time purchase,
- that is owned forever,
- allows for simultaneous readers,
- has no restrictions on printing, and
- can be downloaded as PDFs from within the library community.

Our digital library collections are a great solution to beat the rising cost of textbooks. E-books can be loaded into their course management systems or onto students' e-book readers.
The **Business Expert Press** digital libraries are very affordable, with no obligation to buy in future years. For more information, please visit **www.businessexpertpress.com/librarians**. To set up a trial in the United States, please email **sales@businessexpertpress.com**.

www.ingramcontent.com/pod-product-compliance
Lightning Source LLC
Chambersburg PA
CBHW061316220326
41599CB00026B/4904